METAPHYSICAL REBELLION

METAPHYSICAL REBELLION

Undermining the Void

by Wayne Omura

Bäuu Press
Golden, CO

Copyright © 2020 by Wayne Omura

Without limiting the rights under copyright, no part of this publication may be reproduced, stored in or introduced into a retrieval system, or transmitted, in any form or by any means (electronic, mechanical, photocopying, recording, or otherwise), without the prior written permission of both the copyright owner and the publisher of this book.

ISBN: 978-1-936955-27-5

Layout and typsetting by Nathaniel Kennon Perkins. Front cover art: Doré, Gustave, *The Fall of the Rebel Angels*, 1866.

Published by Bäuu Press
Golden, CO
www.bauuinstitute.com

For the rebels of the heart, the mind, the soul— evolve . . .

CONTENTS

PREFACE ... iii

PART ONE. THE SPIRITUAL REVOLT: REBELLION AGAINST THE GODS ... v

Introduction ... 1
Chapter 1. Revolt of the Angels ... 5
Chapter 2. Faust: Man for Himself ... 29
Chapter 3. Prometheus: A Sacrificial God ... 39

PART TWO. THE EXISTENTIAL REVOLT: REBELLION AGAINST LIFE ... 47

Introduction ... 51
Chapter 4. Vanity of Vanities: Misery and Absurdity in the World of Samuel Beckett ... 53
   Hope in Time While Waiting for Godot: or Salvation from the Muckheap ... 55
Chapter 5. The Tragedy of the Mouse: The Lonely Fate of an Existential Anti-Hero ... 61
Chapter 6. The Stranger: Prophet of Nihilism ... 67
Chapter 7. Nightmare Reality: The Heart of Darkness ... 85

PART THREE. THE METAPHYSICAL REVOLT: REBELLION FOR AUTONOMY ... 93

Introduction ... 95
Chapter 8. The Dream of Life: Kafka and the Quest for Reality ... 97
Chapter 9. Transcendental Nihilism: Life as a Creative Illusion ... 107
Chapter 10. The Philosophy of the Superman: Evolutionary Existentialism ... 115
Chapter 11. The Outsider: Revolution of Meaning ... 125
Chapter 12: Cosmic Laughter: The Transcendental Game of Life ... 135
Chapter 13. Threshold: Evolutionary Consciousness ... 139

Recapitulation ... 141
"The Outer Limits" ... 143

PREFACE

Metaphysical Rebellion—the first step toward transcendence. Man's spirit strives for independence and autonomy. No more bowing down to gods, systems, or dogmas. For the authority must come from within, the decisions must be made by oneself. The strength and courage needed are superhuman, for one is isolated in a world of one's own creation. It is a spiritual breakthrough, an evolution of consciousness, an audacious attempt to become one's own god.

Even in a child one sees this spiritual revolt gestating. Thrust about from situation to situation, forced into activities he can neither stand nor withstand, the child is thwarted in his desires, treated as an object, beaten and threatened into obedience and control. The frustrated toddler cannot fathom the reason for his punishment. All he wants is simply to have what he wants, but these over-sized bullies keep getting in the way. The child cries and stomps his feet, holds his breath and turns blue. But even this blatant outburst achieves no respect. The Rebellion is at its peak. The whole world is against him. All he knows is that something is wrong.

But eventually, like a dog, the child is trained into submission. The spirit is broken. The child must relent. This well-trained animal may never again be free, but rather, spends his remaining life being told what to do (whether by his job, his spouse, his religion, his community, or even his own conscience). And just as with the child, so man's spiritual childhood can be viewed. Throughout history, through legends, literature, mythology and religion, images of defiance herald the awakening of man's soul. From here one can trace the dawn of the revolution, the evolution of man's spiritual consciousness. Such accounts of rebellion reflect the true birth of the free spirit. This indomitable struggle for metaphysical autonomy, this yearning for self-sufficiency, this revolt of the soul may very well be indicative of the innate desire to become God—a self-determining causal agent subservient to no external authority. Will man succeed and advance, or will his spirit be broken like the child's?

Part One: The Spiritual Revolt deals with rebellion on a cosmic scale. These spiritual dissidents defy the divine order and suffer the consequences. Surprisingly, two of these rebel martyrs are not even human.

Part Two: The Existential Revolt concerns the human condition and the human response. The average man on the street—what can he do? The blind alleys, the alienation, can drive one insane.

Part Three: The Metaphysical Revolt lays the choice open before man. He has been handed the power, carte blanche, to do whatever he wants. He has become a god whether he likes it or not. The possibilities are infinite. Man can no longer whine or complain. From this day on he must set things right. He must mold his reality. He must live his dream.

PART ONE

The Spiritual Revolt:
Rebellion Against the Gods

CHAPTER 1.   Revolt of the Angels

CHAPTER 2.   Faust: Man for Himself

CHAPTER 3.   Prometheus: A Sacrificial God

"This will lured me away from God and gods;
for what would there be to create if gods—existed!"[1]

Nietzsche

---

1. Friedrich Nietzsche, *Thus Spoke Zarathustra* (New York: Penguin Books, 1969), p.111.

INTRODUCTION

> "The words of the Preacher, the son
> of David, king in Jerusalem.
> Vanity of vanities, saith the Preacher,
> vanity of vanities; all *is* vanity.
> What profit hath a man of all his
> labour which he taketh under the sun?"
>
> *Ecclesiastes 1:1 – 1:3*

Thus begins the moving account of the most profound essay in the Bible, "Ecclesiastes; or, the Preacher." According to Solomon (the purported author of the book), life is an endlessly repetitive cycle without meaning or purpose, without goal or consequence. Man's lot is therefore to serve God in order to transcend this petty, transient world, this hopeless world utterly devoid of significance, this "vanity of vanities," this "striving after the wind." But is this the only valid conclusion? Is this transcendental resolution the only meaningful path? Could there not be other possible alternatives? Could not value be created out of a valueless void? Cannot man escape the labyrinth of a predestined life?

The anti-heroes, the spiritual revolutionists of Part One, show that meaning can be created independent of an absolute order, that the universe can be significant without a cosmic, teleological structure. Faced with a world of suffering, confusion and despair, humanity can create its own system of values—a Weltanschauung valid by virtue of its autonomy. But to effect such a new order, man must first break with the old order. Man must rebel against the cosmic hierarchy so that he may reign within his own domain. Part One deals with such a spiritual revolt, those rebels with the backbone to challenge the gods.

Chapter One is Satan's rebellion and attempted coup. As a consequence there is a schism—a "Revolt of the Angels." Just because someone is older and more powerful doesn't make him necessarily right—even if the one older and more powerful just happens to be God.

Chapter Two concerns Faust's insatiable desire for knowledge and power. His utilitarian approach leads him into a dubious pact with the Devil. Faust will do anything to become godlike, even going so far as selling his soul. Good or evil, God or Devil—taking sides is irrelevant, for when it comes right down to it, it's every "Man for Himself."

Chapter Three reveals the heroism of a Greek god. Prometheus, with foreknowledge of his tormented fate, still sacrifices himself for love of mankind. He defies all the powers marshaled against him by Olympus. He rebels against the divine order so as to set things right. A lone martyr taking on the entire universe.

The spiritual rebels of Part One make a daring bid for autonomy. They challenge Heaven itself over the destiny of their souls, battling those who interfere with their lives—even if the interference comes from their own maker, from their own god. Despite the gloomy fate of each rebel, their spirits remain free.

Doré, Gustave. *Satan in Council*. c. 1868.

Chapter 1
Revolt of the Angels

"In the beginning God created the heaven and the earth."
—*Genesis 1:1*

From primordial square one man conceives himself not as an independent entity, but rather as dependent upon some external force. Indeed, according to most theological accounts, man himself has not yet entered the scene. A god or force has already shaped reality, determining in advance all possible forms of the world. Man is hence not responsible for his existence, but simply appears on stage under guise of his allotted role. The destiny of mankind has thus been preordained. Man's fate was slavery—born to worship at his Master's feet. However, an alternative factor soon enters into play, infusing man with the spirit of revolt. Curiosity and the temptation of knowledge lead to Adam and Eve's disobedience and "fall" from grace. And yet, the spirit of revolt had existed even prior to man's fall, preceding in many accounts even man himself, originating in that metaphysical netherworld before Creation.

According to the Bible there has been not just one fall from grace, but rather two: one involving man and the other involving angels. Even prior to man's appearance on earth, even prior (in some traditions) to the very existence of the earth, metaphysical rebellion had plagued the tyrannical order of heaven. As a festering gadfly within the hierarchy of the immortals, the spirit of revolt becomes implanted for all time.

The seed takes root through discontent and pride. Tired of standing in attendance, Lucifer is purported to have actually seated himself within the presence of the Almighty, thus aspiring to a position of equality with the Lord. Such impudence results in his being cast down, but not before instigating a "heavenly" revolt with those who are sympathetic, a revolt which causes a schism and subsequent down-"fall" of the angels.

Lucifer, a seraph, the highest of the nine orders of angels, is transformed during the fall into Satan, a monstrous devil. His fellow "angels at arms" are also cast into hell, transforming, as they fall, into hideous demons. Thus, according to many religious accounts, the metaphysical revolt originated long before man was ever conceived— eons before man had ever entered the scene.

The original hero or primary instigator of the rebellion is hence not even human, but rather inhuman—an originally divine rebel ranking supreme among the angels. It is thus Satan, one of the immortals, who takes credit for the original rebellion, for striking the first blow in the cause of metaphysical autonomy—the original paradigm of a spiritual dissident. Satan is therefore not "incarnate evil" as the religious would have us believe, but rather the herald of a new age, the liberator of the soul.

As an angel of the order seraphim it was Lucifer's "privilege" to stand beside the throne of God, singing to the Lord myriad hymns of praise. But such is the role of a dog-servant, and not of a true Being. Thus, Lucifer grows discontent as forbidden thoughts begin to stir, and finally he dares to attempt his own throne. Rather than remaining in attendance subservient to the Lord, Lucifer attempts, not to usurp God's role, but simply to break from the divine hierarchy and to become his own master. But in order to assert his freedom he must necessarily disobey, which leads to a confrontation with the Lord.

God admonishes Lucifer for his pride and his overbearing self-conceit. Lucifer, in turn, disdains God and heaven and thus initiates "the revolt"—a heavenly coup d'etat on behalf of universal freedom. This first act of defiance is only natural for those with dignity and self-esteem, for it is only the weak and cowardly who cringe in self-abasement before their master. Whereas stronger spirits such as Lucifer, cannot help but assert and exercise their free will.

When considering the motives for Lucifer's rebellion, it must be remembered that he is a superior being. Before his fall, Lucifer was acclaimed. He was revered and respected. Not only was Lucifer in the highest order of angels, but he was actually the highest, the most divine, the closest in nature to God. According to most theologians during the time of St. Augustine, "it was generally professed that Lucifer was the most exalted angel in heaven before his fall and transformation into Satan."[2] And according to Jeffrey Russell, an authority on devil scholarship, the liturgical mystery and miracle plays of the Middle Ages esteem Lucifer's status before his fall:

> God made nine orders of angels and created Lucifer the highest angel of the highest order, second in the cosmos only to God himself. God is proud of him: "I have made you closest to me of all the powers; I make you master and mirror of my might; I create you beautiful in bliss, and I name you Lucifer, bearer of light."[3]

According to the second century theologian Tertullian, Lucifer was not only powerful and sublime, but also wise. Jeffrey Russell goes on to explain Tertullian's position:

> Before his fall, he was not only an angel but the foremost angel.... "he was the most eminent of angels, created the wisest of all of them, before he became the Devil."[4]

And Maximillian Rudwin explains that both Jewish and Christian writers exalted Lucifer's status before the fall.

> Lucifer was the chief in the hierarchy of heaven. He was pre-eminent among all created beings in beauty, power and wisdom.... "Thou sealest up the sum, full of wisdom, and perfect in beauty.[5]

And thus, lest we presume to judge and condemn our spiritual superiors, not only does the closest being to God feel the necessity of breaking free, but a host of other angels also follow suit. The urge for freedom and autonomy is contagious, spreading like wildfire

---

2. Henry Ansgar Kelly, *The Devil, Demonology and Witchcraft* (Garden City, New York: Doubleday & Company, Inc., 1968), p. 33.
3. Jeffrey Burton Russell, *Lucifer: The Devil in the Middle Ages* (Ithaca and London: Cornell University Press, 1984), p. 246.
4. Jeffrey Burton Russell, *Satan: The Early Christian Tradition* (Ithaca and London: Cornell University Press, 1981), pp. 92-93.
5. Maximilian Rudwin, *The Devil in Legend and Literature* (Chicago & London: The Open Court Publishing Company, 1931), p. 5.

throughout the rank and file of heaven.

Lucifer is hence responsible for inciting a veritable riot, a civil war between angels, a chain-reaction struggle for power. The warring parties are divided into two camps: those remaining loyal slaves to God and those attempting to gain control of their lives, their destinies, their souls. The sixteenth century physician Johann Wier claims to have determined the exact number of fallen angels. "There were 7,409,127, and they were led by 79 princes."[6] However, this number is in dispute. According to Maximilian Rudwin:

> The number of the angels who participated in this movement of rebellion has never been fully ascertained. The belief current among the Catholic Schoolmen, based upon an interpretation of a biblical phrase (Rev. xii, 4), is that a third of the angels ranged themselves under Satan's standard. The rebel leader's armed force seems to have comprised nearly two thousand four hundred legions (about fourteen million four hundred thousand demons) . . .[7]

However, the attempted "coup" necessarily fails, for the rebel angels are out-numbered two to one. As usual the majority succeeds in thwarting all efforts to advance. And yet the spirit of revolt lingers throughout eternity. The initial revolution fails, but because of their immortality no consummate defeat can be achieved. Thus Satan and his followers are simply banished from heaven, metamorphosing during the Fall into devils and demons.

> And there was war in heaven: Michael and his angels fought against the dragon; and the dragon fought and his angels,
> And prevailed not; neither was their place found any more in heaven.
> And the great dragon was cast out, that old serpent, called the Devil, and Satan, which deceiveth the whole world: he was cast out into the earth, and his angels were cast out with him. (Revelation 12:7 –12:9)

---

6. William Woods, *A History of the Devil* (New York: G.P. Putnam's Sons, 1973), p. 15.
7. Rudwin, *op. cit.*, p. 18.

Heaven temporarily triumphs under the leadership of archangel Michael, yet the spirit of rebellion can never be broken. The Devil and his comrades simply await the next chance, patiently preparing for the opportunity to strike back. Defeat has not crushed, but rather strengthened the resistance. The humiliating exile serves only to fan the fires of revolt. In Milton's famous version, as Satan falls into hell a defiant outcry is heard, a refrain which echoes throughout the spiritual history of the cosmos.

> ...Farewell happy fields,
> Where joy for ever dwells: hail horrors; hail
> Infernal world; and thou profoundest hell
> Receive thy new possessor; one who brings
> A mind not to be changed by place or time.
> The mind is its own place, and in itself
> Can make a heav'n of hell, a hell of heav'n,
> What matter where, if I be still the same,
> And what I should be, all but less than he
> Whom thunder hath made greater? here at least
> We shall be free; th' Almighty hath not built
> Here for his envy, will not drive us hence:
> Here we may reign secure, and in my choice
> To reign is worth ambition, though in hell:
> Better to reign in hell, than serve in heav'n.[8]

Though Satan's attempted "coup" is forestalled, the rebellion is nevertheless a success, for even the power of heaven cannot cope with such pervasive discontent. Satan and his angels are merely shuffled off into the bottomless pit of hell. However, physical confinement cannot imprison the soul, and thus, rather than punishment, the exiles find a kingdom of their own. Although banished into a world of darkness, the divine rebels are at least liberated from the tyranny of their eternal foe. Through defiance they have become autonomous within their own realm. Hence the Devil and his followers have paradoxically won through their defeat. Through their exile they have achieved what they had desired from the start—a world to determine as they themselves

---

8. John Milton, *Paradise Lost and Paradise Regained* (New York: Airmont Publishing Company, Inc., 1968), p. 17.

see fit. The rebel angels are victorious, for although imprisoned in the netherworld, they are at least free.

But once again God sets to work in "his mysterious ways." Frustrated by the celestial anarchy, he is bent upon another of his tyrannical schemes: the creation of a new breed of slaves to replace those who rebelled. But this new breed must lack the capacity for independent thought, for there must be no more disobedience. They must be ignorant and void of will. Thus mankind is born into the world.

Adam and Eve are virtual zombies, automatons following without question the divine, preordained plan. As ignorant slaves before their master, they tend the Lord's garden of Eden. They haven't the slightest qualm or objection, for the role of servitude is all they have ever known—all they are ever allowed to know. In blind obedience and acceptance they do exactly as they are told, for they are "forbidden" the requisite knowledge with which to object.

Satan is incensed by this wanton abuse of power and resolves to undermine the perverted scheme. In the garden of Eden he makes his first successful attempt. If man were to eat of the tree of knowledge his eyes would be opened. His spirit and soul would be freed. Thus, in the cause of enlightenment, the Devil thwarts God's plan. Under guise of a serpent Satan entreats Eve to disobey.

> ... And he said unto the woman, Yea, hath God said, Ye shall not eat of every tree of the garden?
>
> And the woman said unto the serpent, We may eat of the fruit of the trees of the garden:
>
> But of the fruit of the tree which *is* in the midst of the garden, God hath said, Ye shall not eat of it, neither shall ye touch it, lest ye die.
>
> And the serpent said unto the woman, Ye shall not surely die:
>
> For God doth know that in the day ye eat thereof, then your eyes shall be opened, and ye shall be as gods, knowing good and evil.
>
> And when the woman saw that the tree *was* good for food, and that it *was* pleasant to the eyes, and a tree to be desired to make *one* wise, she took of the fruit thereof, and did eat, and gave also unto her husband with her; and he did eat.

Rubens, Peter Paul & Brueghel, Jan, the Elder.
The Garden of Eden with the Fall of Man. c. 1615.

And the eyes of them both were opened . . .
                                      (Genesis 3:1 – 3:7)

And the Lord God said, Behold, the man is become as one of us, to know good and evil . . .
                                      (Genesis 3:22)

Thus God has conspired from the beginning to enslave man in ignorance. Whereas the Devil, the so-called "evil one," the "Prince of Darkness," reveals to man the light of wisdom and knowledge. The attribution of wisdom to the serpent is echoed as late as the New Testament. Jesus himself employs the symbol as he exhorts his disciples: "be ye therefore wise as serpents." (Matthew 10:16)

Thus it is the Devil who liberates man from darkness. Whereas the Lord, in all his benevolence, wishes to restrict man's freedom, suppress man's intellect, and hamper man's growth. God desires, in all his perverseness, for man to remain a child. But Satan, or his familiars (the serpent), intercedes to free man from bondage, propelling him on the path to spiritual maturity. It is thus God, and not the Devil, who is the enemy oppressor of mankind. It is Satan, and not Christ, who is the real savior of the world.

Madam Blavatsky agrees wholeheartedly with this radical reassessment. In her theosophical cosmology, Satan is extolled as a heroic rebel. Jeffrey Russell explains that in Blavatsky's esoteric book *Secret Doctrine*:

> It is the Devil whom we have to thank for our intellects, our wills, and our knowledge, for it was he who opened the blind eyes of the automata that Jehova intended. "Satan, the serpent of Genesis, [is] the real creator and benefactor, the Father of Spiritual Mankind."[9]

In a similar manner the French novelist, George Sand, believes that the attributes of God and Satan have been reversed. In her novel, *Consuelo*, she clears up this distortion, this perverted myth.

> In the opinion of the Lollards, Satan was not the enemy of the human race, but on the contrary its protector and

---

9. Jeffrey Burton Russell, *Mephistopheles: The Devil in the Modern World* (Ithaca and London: Cornell University Press, 1986), p. 219.

patron. They held that he was a victim to injustice and jealousy. According to them the archangel Michael, and the other celestial powers who had precipitated him into the abyss, were the real demons, while Lucifer, Beelzebub, Ashtaroth, Astarte, and all the monsters of hell, were innocence and light themselves.[10]

The Devil and his cohorts are hence the allies of man. God and the "heavenly" angels are humanity's worst foe. Satan incites man to disobedience, offering wisdom and knowledge as consolation. Man accepts the temptation which, according to the Lord, is a sin, for it raises man's consciousness to that of God. And so, through Adam and Eve's transgression and fall from grace, heaven once more suffers a humiliating defeat. God's will has again been undermined by Satan who comes to the rescue by awakening man's soul. And thus William Woods explains the derivation of his name:

> He was not only Satan. He was also, as the earliest prophets were perceptive enough to understand, Lucifer, the bearer of light, the spur to curiosity and thus to knowledge.[11]

Man has lost his innocence and become capable of evil. Yet he has also gained the right to consciously choose such evil. Man is thus responsible, whether or not he accepts the responsibility. He is no longer a zombie, but rather a fully conscious human being. In such a way Satan has "shown man the light"—leading him as a beacon out of a spiritual abyss. Having lost his divine childhood man has now become the veritable spawn of the Devil—allies against the tyranny of God.

Eighteenth-century romanticism carried on the banner of the revolution. It adopted and proclaimed the theological reversal of roles: Satan representing the force of light, God representing the force of darkness. The entire romantic movement, up to and including the twentieth century, has more or less justified the Satanic revolt. Romanticism, being a movement which glorifies individual

---

10. George Sand, *Consuelo* (New York: A.L. Burt, Publisher, 1900), pp. 231-232.
11. William Woods, *A History of the Devil* (New York: G.P. Putnam's Sons, 1973), p. 13.

subjectivity, would naturally support any rebellion for autonomy. Hence:

> During the period of the Romantic revolt in all European countries Satan was considered as a Prometheus of Christian mythology. He was hailed as the vindicator of reason, of freedom of thought, and of an unfettered humanity. The French Romantics saw in Satan the greatest enthusiast for the liberty and spontaneity of genius, the sublimest and supremest incarnation of the spirit of individualism, the greatest symbol of protest against tyranny, celestial or terrestrial.[12]

The necessary correlate to the glorification of Satan is the inevitable damnation of God and heaven. Man's spiritual revolt passed from Europe to America as is evident in the classical writings of Mark Twain. This blasphemous author portrays the Lord under various possible guises: a reckless, thoughtless, merciless force; a malevolent deity; and what is perhaps the worst of all—a simple illusion. In his last, unfinished novel, *The Mysterious Stranger*, Twain writes a diatribe against the insanity of God, a god, according to Satan:

> . . . who mouths justice, and invented hell—mouths mercy, and invented hell—mouths Golden Rules, and forgiveness multiplied by seventy times seven, and invented hell; who mouths morals to other people, and has none himself; who frowns upon crimes, yet commits them all; who created man without invitation . . . and finally, with altogether divine obtuseness, invites this poor abused slave to worship him![13]

The question is whether the Lord and his angels are really guilty of criminal acts. If so, then perhaps Satan is justified in his role as "the accuser." In fact, the name "Satan" itself means not only "devil" and "adversary," but "It is generally accepted that the name 'Satan' comes from the verb śātan, 'to persecute, be hostile to' and, also, more

---

12. Rudwin, *op. cit.* p. 15.
13. Mark Twain, *The Mysterious Stranger* (Berkeley and Los Angeles: University of California Press, 1969), p. 405.

specifically, 'to accuse.' "[14] Thus Satan may be the only force of justice in the universe. If God is indeed guilty of immorality, then the Devil may in fact be the only advocate of man.

The linguistic derivation of the word "devil" also poses questions and doubts. Devil: "fr. Gk *diabolos*, lit., slanderer, fr. *diaballein* to throw across, discredit, slander."[15] What is it that the Devil is attempting to discredit? The answer is obviously the forces of heaven and God. The Devil assumes the role of an adversary to the Lord, and consequently, dogmatic assumptions label him an enemy of man. But is this classical interpretation necessarily true? Is it not possible that Satan is the benefactor, and that God and all his angels are the tyrannical oppressors of humanity? If so, then the Devil is the veritable "bearer of light." And such is the exact meaning of one of his many appellatives. Lucifer: "ME *lucifer* morning star & *Lucifer* fallen rebel archangel, devil, fr. OE, fr. L *lucifer* morning star, fr. *lucifer*, adj., light-bearing (prob. trans. of Gk phōsphoros light-bearing, morning star)."[16] Thus Lucifer, a name synonymous with the Devil, is even more clearly of a positive origin. Is it simply an inexplicable paradox or could it be an appropriate title? Theologians argue that the meaning refers only to Lucifer's nature *before* the fall. But staunch and determined Romantics maintain that the meaning of Lucifer is symbolic for only *after* the fall.

A similar paradox arises out of the derivation of the word "demon." "Demon" derived from the Latin "daemon" which in turn derived from the Greek word "daimōn." The meaning of daimōn shifted through the centuries from a godlike entity; to a neutral spiritual being ambiguous in character and intermediate in rank between the gods and man; to an overtly hostile and malicious entity bent upon the corruption and damnation of man. The shift in connotation was slow but sure, as Jeffrey Russell explains:

> In the *Iliad*, *daimōn* is frequently used as an equivalent of *theos*. In the *Odyssey*, the term has more frequent negative than positive connotations but is still ambiguous. . . . By the late Hellenistic period the term *daimonion* had

---

14. Rivkah Schärf Kluger, *Satan in the Old Testament* (Evanston: Northwestern University Press, 1967), p.25.
15. *Webster's Third New International Dictionary* (Springfield: G. & C. Merrian Company, 1961), p. 618.
16. *Ibid.*, p. 1343.

acquired an almost universally bad connotation.[17]

Thus "demon" was originally used interchangeably with the word "theos" or god. And what's more, "Plato says the name is derived from *daemon = knowing*, as they were possessed of greater intelligence than the human race."[18] Thus the negative term "demon" originally typified a somewhat positive character, but gradually became identified with a wholly malevolent entity. The transformation is suspect considering the unbridled censorship of theologians. In fact Plato's own pupil, Xenocrates, was responsible for completing the distortion, shifting all negative qualities onto demons, all positive qualities onto gods.

Could it be possible that demons are exactly as their linguistic derivation describes them: spiritual beings superior to man? Could Satan, Lucifer, and the Devil be victims of slander—nothing in their "God-given" facades remaining true but their names? The question may be more important than the answer, for the problem can never be resolved. However the question itself forces us to re-evaluate the Lord, and such re-evaluation results in a totally negative divine portrait. Consequently a powerful intellectual enlightenment occurred during the twentieth century which insidiously undermined the faith in God. This trend in modern society toward agnosticism, existentialism, and atheism resulted from the blasphemies and heretical doctrines of metaphysical rebels. English philosopher, Bertrand Russell, an agnostic, playfully joins in the attack. In his most famous essay, "A Free Man's Worship," Russell depicts God as a veritable fiend:

> To Dr. Faustus in his study Mephistophelis told the history of the Creation, saying:
> "The endless praises of the choirs of angels had begun to grow wearisome; for, after all, did he not deserve their praise? Had he not given them endless joy? Would it not be more amusing to obtain underserved praise, to be worshipped by beings whom he tortured? He smiled inwardly, and resolved that the great drama should be performed."[19]

---

17. Jeffrey Burton Russell, *The Devil: Perceptions of Evil from Antiquity to Primitive Christianity* (Ithaca, New York: Cornell University Press, 1977), p. 142.
18. J. Charles Wall, *Devils* (Detroit: Singer Tree Press, 1968), p. 9.
19. Bertrand Russell, "A Free Man's Worship" from *The Basic Writings of Bertrand Russell* (New York: Simon and Schuster, 1961), p. 66.

The problem is whether God is as dark as Russell and the romantics portray him. While it is generally acknowledged that the God of the Old Testament is stern and vindictive, this is always justified as the result of the barbarity of the times. The Lord was severe in his punishment, so the apology goes, because man himself was akin to a malicious child. As man himself was brutal and savage he only respected force. Consequently God, by necessity, also had to appear malevolent, if only in order to teach man a lesson. Thus the defense runs in order to justify divine crimes. But to the metaphysical rebels this wanton savagery is unacceptable.

With the Bible as evidence, the Almighty appears as a sadistic tyrant. He seemingly gains pleasure from manipulating and destroying human life. But the cruelty is excessive. The punishment far outweighs the rewards. For as the character Ivan explains in Dostoyevsky's last novel, *The Brothers Karamozov,* even eternal paradise cannot atone for the suffering of one innocent child. In the chapter (appropriately entitled "Rebellion") which is the prelude to the famous "Grand Inquisitor" scene, Ivan argues with his brother Alyosha who is a monk. If the price of admission to paradise is the unjust suffering of even one child, then it is too much to pay.

> "It's not that I don't accept God, Alyosha, I just most respectfully return him the ticket."
> "That is rebellion," Alyosha said softly, dropping his eyes.[20]

But what other course is there to take? The God of the Old Testament is not concerned with man's welfare, but rather with brutally flaunting his might. The question is whether these accusations against God can be proven. Are Twain, Russell, and Dostoyevsky correct in their divine assessment, or are they over-reacting to a few minor incidents? To resolve this problem the Bible itself must be consulted.

The books of the Old Testament abound with acts of depravity, violence, rape, and murder—all apparently carried out under the auspices of the Lord. The Almighty, in all his justice and mercy, simply grants Israel a homeland and orders the extermination of the native inhabitants. The massacre is executed as per divine commandment.

---

20. Fyodor Dostoevsky, *The Brothers Karamazov* (San Francisco: North Point Press, 1990), p. 245.

Israel invades and totally annihilates all kingdoms, all civilizations, all peoples of the promised land. Joshua leads Israel against Jericho in the first phase of the attack:

> And they utterly destroyed all that *was* in the city, both man and woman, young and old, and ox, and sheep, and ass, with the edge of the sword. . . .
> And they burnt the city with fire, and all that *was* therein. . .
> So the Lord was with Joshua; and his fame was *noised* throughout all the country. (Joshua 6:21 – 6:27)

Thus God is not only responsible, but actually takes pride in the genocidal murder of thousands of men, women, and children—people whose sole crime was to be living in the wrong place. Slaughter and bloodshed are apparently a matter of distinction in the eyes of the Lord. Destruction being the solution for those who stand in the way. But is this wanton tyranny divine justice? Apparently so in the omniscient eyes of heaven. Thus the destruction continues:

> And *so* it was, *that* all that fell that day, both of men and women, *were* twelve thousand, *even* all the men of Ai.
> For Joshua drew not his hand back, wherewith he stretched out the spear, until he had utterly destroyed all the inhabitants of Ai. . . .
> And Joshua burnt Ai, and made it an heap forever, *even* a desolation unto this day. (Joshua 8:25 – 8:28)

The slaughter increases at an alarming rate. The destruction becomes so rampant that the accounts are generalized.

> So Joshua smote all the country of the hills, and of the south, and of the vale, and of the springs, and all their kings: he left none remaining, but utterly destroyed all that breathed, as the Lord God of Israel commanded. (Joshua 10:40)

Joshua, leading Israel, destroys approximately 55 kingdoms along with all their inhabitants. The number of murders probably runs into the hundreds of thousands as Israel conquers the divinely promised land. The objection could be made that these were the actions of a single, demented leader distorting the words of God. But even after Joshua's death the slaughter continues with renewed vigor under new leaders of Israel, new servants of the Lord:

> And Judah went up; and the Lord delivered the Canaanites and the Perizites into their hand: and they slew of them in Bezek ten thousand men.(Judges 1:4)

> And Saul smote the Amalekites from Havilah *until* thou comest to Shur, that *is* over against Egypt.
> . . . and utterly destroyed all the people with the edge of the sword. (I Samuel 15:7 – 15:8)

David invades and destroys three nations. "And David smote the land, and left neither man nor woman alive . . ." (I Samuel 27:9)

> And the Syrians fled before Israel; and David slew *the men of* seven hundred chariots of the Syrians, and forty thousand horsemen . . . (II Samuel 10:18)

Thus the pattern is established for centuries to come. The Lord commands and Israel destroys. The slaughter of innocents runs literally into the millions as each king of the Jewish people partakes of his share of the murder. The objection can be raised that each leader may well have mistaken the words of the Lord, that each king may have distorted God's will. But the Bible itself clearly contradicts this view:

> Thus saith the Lord of hosts . . .
> Now go and smite Amalek, and utterly destroy all that they have and spare them not; but slay both man and woman, infant and suckling, ox and sheep, camel and ass. (I Samuel 15:2 – 15:3)

Hence it is God himself who exhorts the people of Israel to commit genocide. Eventually, after successive victories, even "God's chosen" begin to tire of the slaughter. Slowly, with increasing confidence and security, the Israelites begin to show mercy to their enemies, and this is in blatant defiance of the Lord.

> And it came to pass, when Israel was strong, that they put the Canaanites to tribute, and did not utterly drive them out....
>
> Neither did Zebulun drive out the inhabitants of Kitron, nor the inhabitants of Nahalol; but the Canaanites dwelt among them, and became tributaries. (Judges 1:28 – 1:30)

And yet whenever Israel begins to show kindness and tolerance, heaven is quick to rebuke. It is apparently the divine will to transform the Israelites into ruthless murderers. It is apparently the will of God to make war and not peace, to devastate civilizations willing to coexist, not only in harmony, but even in subservience.

> And an angel of the Lord came up from Gilgal to Bochim, and said . . .
>
> And ye shall make no league with the inhabitants of this land; ye shall throw down their altars: but ye have not obeyed my voice: why have ye done this? (Judges 2:1 – 2:2)

Thus the people of Israel are upbraided for making peace with the inhabitants of the promised land. Rather than annihilation they allow them to reside in harmony. And this is apparently a great sin against God—a supposedly kind and loving, benevolent God!

An earlier incident further illustrates God's mania for destruction. In "Numbers," the Lord commands Moses to send Israel against the Midianites. The war is fought as per divines orders, Israel engaging with twelve thousand troops. With divine assistance they are victorious and slay the Midianite men, but:

> . . . the children of Israel took *all* the women of Midian captives, and their little ones . . .
>
> And Moses was wroth with the officers of the host . . .
>
> And Moses said unto them, Have ye saved all the women alive?
>
> Behold, these caused the children of Israel . . . to commit trespass against the Lord . . .
>
> Now therefore kill every male among the little ones, and kill every woman that hath known man by lying with him.

> But all the women children, that have not known a man by lying with him, keep alive for yourselves. (Numbers 31:9 – 31:18)

And so thousands of innocent male babies, toddlers, and young boys are put to the sword. Thousands more of women, wives, and elderly grandmothers are also slain. Of the remaining 32,000 Midianite virgins, half are given over to be enjoyed by the soldiers, half are given to be used by the people, 32 are given to the priest, and 32 are given to the Levites who keep charge of the tabernacle of the Lord. Thus human beings are treated as, and even referred to as "booty"—spoils to be divided up and enjoyed by the victors. The superfluous, the males and the non-virgin women, are simply disposed of as so much trash. God is thus opposed to the demonstration of mercy, demanding instead the ruthless exploitation of all under his sway. Hence, heaven trains Israel not in the cultivation of "goodness," but rather in the art of merciless, brute force.

In this manner the Bible abounds with acts of violence and murder, corruption and depravity, decadence and evil. And such evil is carried out under the banner of the Lord! However, the argument can be made that such are the acts of man and not God, or at worst the results of man's misinterpretation of the Lord. Such apologies claim God to be innocent and man the sole repository of guilt, but though such arguments can be made, they cannot be sustained. For the Bible is replete with acts of depravity committed solely by the Lord. One has only to recall the incident of the Flood where God drowns the population of earth by inundating the planet 150 days in water.

> And all the flesh died that moved upon the earth, both of fowl, and of cattle, and of beast, and of every creeping thing that creepeth upon the earth, and every man:
> All in whose nostrils *was* the breath of life, of all that *was* in the dry *land*, died.
> And every living substance was destroyed which was upon the face of the ground . . . (Genesis 7:21 – 7:23)

This destruction of life on a planetary scale contrasts with trivial incidents of retaliation and vindictiveness. These more specific acts of private vengeance are conveniently glossed over by biblical scholars.

> And Er, Judah's firstborn, was wicked in the sight of the Lord; and the Lord slew him.
> And Judah said unto Onan, Go in unto thy brother's wife, and marry her, and raise up seed to thy brother.
> And Onan knew that the seed should not be his; and it came to pass, when he went in unto his brother's wife, that he spilled *it* on the ground, lest that he should give seed to his brother.
> And the thing which he did displeased the Lord: wherefore he slew him also. (Genesis 38:7 – 38:10)

Thus God is not above the level of petty violence, but is quick to appease his pride, his desire for vengeance for disobedience.

Once again, in the plagues against Egypt, God intervenes to destroy thousands of innocent lives: firstborn Egyptians sacrificed to show the power of the Lord. At first sight God might not appear entirely to blame, for the sacrifice was ostensibly necessary to free Israel from Egypt. And yet time after time the Pharaoh was ready to relent and set Israel free, but the Lord God "hardened his heart" so that the show might go on. And thus God proclaims in a typically pompous manner:

> For I will pass through the land of Egypt this night, and will smite all the first born in the land of Egypt, both man and beast; and against all the gods of Egypt I will execute judgement: I *am* the Lord. (Exodus 12:12)
> And it came to pass, that at midnight the Lord smote all the firstborn in the land of Egypt . . . (Exodus 12:29)

Thus the slaughter committed by God is of cold and calculated first degree mass murder. And the bloodshed escalates throughout human history. Even the Israelites themselves are not immune from the slaughter. In the first book of "Samuel" (6:19) God murders 50,070 of the Jewish people simply because they dared to look into the ark of the covenant. The fatalities on both sides climb to a staggering degree. In the second book of "Kings" (19:35) an angel of the Lord ventures forth and slays 185,000 Assyrians in their sleep. In the second book of "Chronicles" (13:17) God directs the slaying of a half million Israelites as punishment for their idolatry. The list of divine atrocities is seemingly endless. The Lord God is truly the first serial mass-murderer. And while the severity of the punishment grows, the triviality of the crimes makes God look like a petty, loathsome monster—in fact, more of a devil than the Devil himself. Witness the insanity of the retribution in the second book of "Kings" (2:23 – 2:24):

> And he went up from thence into Bethel: and as he was going up by the way, there came forth little children out of the city, and mocked him, and said unto him, Go up, thou bald head; go up, thou bald head.
> And he turned back, and looked on them, and cursed them in the name of the Lord. And there came forth two she bears out of the wood, and tare forty and two children of them.

Forty-two innocent children are torn to pieces simply for making fun of one of the prophets of the Lord. Is it any wonder that the inhabitants of the promised land are faint with fear? For the ruthless invaders are apparently blessed by God. Hence there appears something of a reversal of roles: God on the side of evil opposing the forces of good. In Joshua 2:9 the harlot, Rahab, betrays Jericho, for she knows the city is doomed.

> ... I know that the Lord hath given you the land, and that your terror is fallen upon us, and that all the inhabitants of the land faint because of you.

Thus Israel dominates through terror, murder, and destruction. They oppress everyone, and their "fame is *noised* throughout the land." In "Judges" 18:7 & 18:27 Israel destroys an advanced and peaceful society. Apparently God's will is with the warmongers and opposed to the civilized. Israel, sending forth spies unto the kingdom of Laish,

> ... saw the people that *were* therein, how they dwelt careless, after the manner of the Zidonians, quiet and secure; and *there was* no magistrate in the land, that might put *them* to shame in *any* thing; and they *were* far from the Zidonians, and had no business with *any* man.

The troops of Israel advance,

> . . . and came upon Laish, unto a people *that were* at quiet and secure: and they smote them with the edge of the sword, and burnt the city with fire.

Hence, God and his "chosen" are the barbarians, the rest of humanity the victims. God the oppressor, mankind the oppressed. Is it then possible that God is not only homicidal but also genocidal?—that God is the force of evil and Satan the force of good? From the Bible it becomes clear that the Lord is a considerable cause of human suffering. Whereas Satan, on the other hand, is an unassuming character who stands to the side.

God and his minions prove their malevolence, a malevolence which manifests in an outward appearance of horror. In "Judges" 13:6 reference is made that the countenance of an angel of God is "very terrible." In "Judges" 13:22 the sight of the Lord is so frightening that people think they will die if they see him. In the first book of "Samuel" 16:15 reference is made to "an evil spirit from God." Thus the spirits of the Lord are themselves described as being evil. And if any doubt still remains, the following are only a few references to the decadent nature of God:

> "O Lord God of heaven, the great and terrible God . . ." (Nehemiah 1:5)

> " . . . remember the Lord, *which* is great and terrible . . ." (Nehemiah 4:14)

> " . . . our God, the great, the mighty, and the terrible God . . ." (Nehemiah 9:32)

> " . . . with God *is* terrible majesty . . ." (Job 37:22)

> "Men do therefore fear him: he respecteth not any *that are* wise of heart." (Job 37:24)

> "Serve the Lord with fear, and rejoice with trembling. Kiss the Son, lest he be angry, and ye perish *from* the way, when his wrath is kindled but a little." (Psalms 2:11 – 2:12)

> " . . . and they bowed their heads, and worshipped the

Lord with *their* faces to the ground." (Nehemiah 8:6)

Is there any wonder that Satan and his angels rebelled against this tyrannical and "demonic" God? The forces of heaven are obviously out to oppress mankind, to force man into spiritual submission. Whereas Satan, on the other hand, is out to free humanity, to set man on the pathway of spiritual growth. But this liberation can only be effected through the dissemination of knowledge. Lucifer must then literally show man the light! And he does so to the great displeasure of the Lord. Thus the Devil is in fact the first metaphysical rebel, the first autonomous hero in defiance of God.

> Satan rebelled, he refused to serve, he refused to transmit his divine message, he wished to become original, the author of his own destiny, the bearer of his own light. And immediately, by the very laws of being, he "fell" from Heaven, which is the Realm where God's intention reigns absolute. He became his own messenger, and as he is but a pure spirit, once the source of the Spirit was cut off, he became the messenger of Nothingness and its mysteries.[21]

In his metaphysical novel, *The Revolt of the Angels*, Anatole France tells the story of a second angelic revolt. A band of dissident, fallen angels renew an attempted overthrow of "Ialdabaoth," the Biblical God now revealed as pure evil. The angels plead with Satan, the archetypal rebel, to lead them once again against the forces of heaven. Satan hesitates, then tells them his answer. That night, in a dream, Satan has a vision. Ialdabaoth is overthrown and Satan himself is set in the place of God. Gradually he sees himself becoming just as loathsome, petty, intolerant, and in short, just as despicable as the previous God. Satan awakens from his dream in an icy sweat. Calling the rebel leaders to counsel, the majestic angel gives them their answer. The war is to be called off, for

> ...War engenders war, and victory defeat.
> God, conquered, will become Satan; Satan, conquering, will become God. May the fates spare me this terrible lot;

---

21. Denis de Rougemont, *The Devil's Share* (New York: Pantheon Books, 1944), p. 31.

I love the Hell which formed my genius.[22]

Satan explains that he loves the earth and wants to remain and help humanity. What's more, the rebel angels must realize that by destroying ignorance and fear, superstition and falsehood, they have already succeeded in defeating Ialdabaoth. Satan tells his fellow comrades that the only way to destroy God's power, to counter the malign forces of heaven, is to remain on earth and preach love and kindness, art and beauty to all mankind. Thus they would surely reign victorious by engendering peace and harmony between the forces of good and evil, earth and heaven. By triumphing over themselves they would triumph over God. In the inspiring conclusion of the novel Satan speaks of the original fall of the angels.

> "We were conquered because we failed to understand that Victory is a Spirit, and that it is in ourselves and in ourselves alone that we must attack and destroy Ialdabaoth."[23]

Thus the transformation is complete: God is really the Devil, the Devil is really God. In order to save himself, man must become symbolically allied to Satan. For otherwise his soul will fall prey to divine tyranny. Whether or not God and Satan even exist is academic. For, even if only a myth, it is on the side of the Devil that those partaking in the Metaphysical Rebellion must stand. Wisdom, knowledge, strength of will, spiritual autonomy—it is only by nurturing these "devilish" qualities that man will evolve and "transcend."

---

22. Anatole France, *The Revolt of the Angels* (New York: The Heritage Press, 1953), p. 282.
23. *Ibid.*, p. 282.

"*If* there were gods, how could I endure not to be a god! *Hence* there are no gods."[24]

> Nietzsche

---

24. Friedrich Nietzsche, *Thus Spoke Zarathustra* from *The Portable Nietzsche* (New York: Penguin Books, 1982), p. 198.

Jacomin, Alfred-Louis. *Faust and Mephistopheles*. 1869.

Chapter 2
Faust: Man for Himself

"Here is the spirit free, The mind exalted..."[25]

—Goëthe

With traditional values awry where can man turn? With God being a devil and Satan being a god, whom can man trust? The historic alliance man had with God ends with man betrayed. A similar alliance with Satan may very well end the same. The prudent man will trust no one. Faith and trust belong nowhere but with oneself.

Faust follows this creed in an exemplary manner. He believes and trusts no one but himself. What he wants is knowledge and power, and he will employ any means to achieve this end. Even going so far as to forfeit his soul.

In Dorothy Sayers' version of Faust, *The Devil to Pay*, Faust is tormented by the dichotomy of good and evil, or rather, what is traditionally considered to be good and evil. The God-Satan reversal of roles is the key to Faust's initial pact with Lucifer. Faust allies himself with Mephistopheles so that with his increased powers he can help mankind, but mankind quickly turns against him.

> O men, men! Why will you quarrel and fight? Why seek to harm me, that have only loved you and labored for your good? I would free you from the burden of fear and pain and poverty that God has laid upon you.... Be men!

---

25. Johann Wolfgang von Göethe, *Faust* (undetermined translation and reference).

> Rouse yourselves! Throw off this bondage of superstition, and learn to know your friends from your foes. I am not your enemy. God is the enemy of us all—[26]

But mankind remains stubborn and so Faust gives up. Why try to help people who are content with their suffering, with worshipping a false god? And so Faust forgoes his altruism and seeks only what pleases himself.

Sayers ends her version with a traditional Christian theme. Man for himself becomes corrupt and debauched. Faust repents although it may or may not do him any good. His hope and faith and love for God are all that matter.

The countless versions of the Faust legend have a basic theme. Whether ending with a religious, moralistic stance as with Sayers, or ending with the spiritual rebellion of the romantics, the underlying premise is the same. Faust is the drama of man's soul torn between good and evil, struggling for power and self-enhancement. It is an archetypal image of human consciousness. It is the story of man's quest for understanding—in a sense a "Bildungsroman," a romantic search for identity, an education novel on a cosmic scale.

"I will know, or I will not live,"[27] rages Faust to Mephostophiles in the original Faustbook printed by Johann Spies. The original version, written in the sixteenth century, depicts a curious, ambitious, and yet foolhardy Faust who is in league with the Devil. For twenty-four years Mephostophiles will grant his every wish. But at the end of the allotted time Faust will lose his soul. The pact is signed in blood (twice for good measure). And there is no way out. Faust's quest for knowledge and power will be his doom.

Even Mephostophiles wearies of Faust's incessant questioning:

> Faustus (quoth the Spirit) I am loth to reason with thee any further, for thou art never satisfied in thy mind . . .[28]

---

26. Dorothy L. Sayers, *The Devil to Pay* (London: Victor Gollancz Ltd., 1939), pp. 51-52.
27. William Rose (editor), *The Historie of the Damnable Life and Deserved Death of Doctor John Faustus* (Notre Dame: University of Notre Dame Press, 1963), p. 91.
28. *Ibid.*, pp. 96-97.

The problem is that the more Faust learns, the more he regrets what he has done. He realizes that he has sacrificed and condemned his soul. He wants to back out, but his increased knowledge (backed by Lucifer's threats) makes him realize that it is too late.

Mephostophiles, himself, says Faust should never have signed the pact. For what is twenty-four years to an eternity of damnation. But Faust had been stubborn. He wanted power. He wanted to know.

> ... therefore give none the blame but thine own self-will, thy proud and aspiring mind, which hath brought thee into the wrath of God and utter damnation.[29]

Time passes. Faust learns everything he wants to know. He has every desire fulfilled, even having Helen of Troy as his lover. He plays tricks, goes on adventures, shows off, carouses with his cohorts. Mephostophiles is at his beck and call. But all too soon the twenty-four years draw to a close. In the end Faust's body is found torn apart with his brains splattered all around. The Devil exacts his due. Faust's soul is doomed.

Moral? In this anonymous Lutheran version—one should avoid the temptation of evil. Too much knowledge and power does no one good. The secrets of life are better left unknown. The result of tampering with fate and conspiring against God is eternal damnation.

But even in this original, moralistic version something about Faust strikes a sympathetic chord. A universal archetype seems to resound through the Faustian theme. Man for himself? Man into god? The child who wants everything? In Christopher Marlowe's version, Faust charges Mephostophilis to demand of Lucifer under the pact:

> Letting him live in all voluptuousness,
> Having thee ever to attend on me,
> To give me whatsoever I shall ask;
> To tell me whatsoever I demand:
> To slay mine enemies, and aid my friends,
> And always be obedient to my will.[30]

Such conditions reek of a power-mad dictator, a spoiled child, or an immature god. Marlowe's drama closely follows the original Faustbook

---
29. *Ibid.*, pp. 97-98.
30. Christopher Marlow, *Doctor Faustus* (New York: Hill and Wang, 1965), p. 19.

and departs little from its religious, censorious theme. Faust is shown to be mistaken, to have reaped the damnation he deserved, and yet somehow the reader sympathizes with his plight. Is it because everyone secretly desires the powers Faust attained? Is it because deep inside each and every one of us is a budding Faust? Fausts who are too timid to pay the price of godhood—the gambling of one's soul? If given half a chance wouldn't everyone be tempted by the knowledge and power of Faust? For who among us believes in eternal damnation anyway?

Because Faust is essentially the story of every man's soul, the German poet Heinrich Heine writes: "Jeder Mensch sollte einen Faust schreiben."[31] "Every man should write a Faust." And he himself did—from his deathbed. *Doktor Faust: A Dance Poem* is a ballet based upon scenes from the original Faust legend. Heine varied little from the plot and theme of the original Faust. His originality lies in transcribing the words and story into visual displays and movements. The significance of Heine's *Dance Poem* is that it was lost and re-surfaced, that it was his last major work, and that it was written while his own soul was suffering and contending with death.

"Every man should write a Faust." But not everyone can. Although the Faust archetype transcends culture and time, few follow its path. The Faustian character is of a Nietzschean, superman cast. Average souls may be tempted, but they play it safe and turn back. In Thomas Mann's *Doctor Faustus* the narrator speaks of the immeasurable distance between the young Faust (Adrian Leverkühn) and all his peers:

> I felt, not without a pang, the foreordained gulf between his existence and that of these striving and high-purposed youths. It was the difference of the life-curve between good, yes, excellent average, which was destined to return from that roving, seeking student life to its bourgeois courses, and the other, invisibly singled out, who would never forsake the hard route of the mind, would tread it, who knew whither, and whose gaze, whose attitude, never quite resolved in the fraternal, whose inhibitions in his personal relations made me and probably others aware that he himself divined this difference.[32]

---

31. J.W. Smeed, *Faust in Literature* (London: Oxford University Press, 1975), p. 1.
32. Thomas Mann, *Doctor Faustus* (New York: Random House, Inc., 1948), p. 126.

Retzsch, Friedrich August Moritz.
The Chess Players or The Game of Life. c. 1831.

"Driven" is the word that characterizes the Faustian spirit. Whether one is driven toward excellence (as in Mann's musical genius Adrian Leverkühn) or toward knowledge (as in Göethe's *Faust*).

Göethe provided the turning point in man's acceptance of the Faust archetype. At last, with Göethe's drama, Faust is seen in a positive light. What is admirable about Faust is honestly expressed, not only by Göethe and humanity, but by God himself. In the prologue to his drama, which smacks uncannily of Job, the Lord and Mephistopheles debate over the strengths and weaknesses of Faust. Mephistopheles bets that he can lead Faust astray, and the Lord confidently agrees to the wager:

> So be it; I shall not forbid it!
> Estrange this spirit from its primal source,
> Have licence, if you can but win it,
> To lead it down your path by shrewd resource;
> And stand ashamed when you must own perforce:
> A worthy soul through the dark urge within it
> Is well aware of the appointed course.[33]

The drama unfolds. Faust becomes entangled in romance and intrigue. He commits murder. Is swayed from the noble path. But eventually in old age he returns to his true course. According to Göethe, the true course is striving for the good and creatively helping mankind.

Faust is in danger of losing his soul to the Devil. He has lost his wager by saying "Yes" to life. But a double wager on Faust's soul had existed between Mephistopheles and the Lord. If Faust ended his life debauched, Mephistopheles could take him. If Faust ended his life with nobility, he would be the Lord's. Faust's affirmation of life was his joy in creatively assisting his fellow men. The Lord's confidence in Faust proved out in the end. A host of angels arrives to bear Faust off to Heaven. In the inspiring and lofty conclusion to Göethe's romantic drama, the angels proclaim:

> Pure spirits' peer, from evil coil

---

33. Johann Wolfgang von Göethe, *Faust: A Tragedy* (New York: W.W. Norton & Company, Inc., 1976), p. 8.

> He was vouchsafed exemption;
> "Whoever strives in ceaseless toil,
> Him we may grant redemption"[34]

Göethe ends his masterpiece with an encouraging reversal of the traditional Faust theme. Instead of damnation, Faust finds salvation. The message, the moral (out of the mouths of angels): one may stray, and one may err, but as long as one strives and aspires and never gives up—one can always find redemption.

In general, the Faust legend is an archetype of a man who goes all out for himself. In defiance of God, or man, or even the Devil himself, Faust's primary concern is to serve his own interests and purpose. "Me first" is his philosophical dictum. In a similar manner criminals, murderers, anarchists, and transgressors all do the same. They break societal laws. But who cares what's good for society? In the final analysis it's every man for himself. Faust realized this basic metaphysical truth, and unlike others he acted upon it to the very end, regardless of the fate of his soul. It's Faust's courage and single-mindedness that deserve respect.

In an obscure, but perhaps most inspiring version of the Faust legend, this "me first" dictum is honed to the ultimate. Man's most important virtue is seen as his independence, his autonomy. In the play, *Mr. Faust*, Arthur Ficke presents an unusual twist to the Faustian legend.

Satan is shown to be merely a pawn of the Lord. His duty is to tempt man toward evil and rebellion only to turn the tables in the end, proving the futility of such a path. The Devil and God were both in on the trick from the start. But Faust is unmoved. Who cares if the whole world is against him? What does it matter if all creation laughs at his cause? Till his last dying breath he will never relent. For to be God's slave is not in his heart.

> Faust.
>   ... Wherefore I still shall seek
>   In life itself my refuge: not in God;
>   [Turning to the altar]
>   And cry: "With all its bitterness on my head,
>   My Will be done, not Thy Will!"

---

34. *Ibid.*, p. 303.

Brander.
>Blasphemy!
>Ah, Faust, what madness! . . .

Faust.
>I go into a darkness past your thought.
>. . . My last altar lies
>Smoking in ruins; and I stand alone
>Of all the universe. But my Will be done!
>My errant tortured Will, my bitter Will,
>My Will, my Will![35]

Ficke ends his play in an almost sophomoric manner with an adoring woman caring for Faust more than she does for her own husband. Is it true that the courageous, lone wolf wins the wife of the sheepish husband? Ficke implies "yes," although in everyday life the outcome is arguable. But even if Ficke is right, does this not, in itself, detract from the purpose of the rebellion? If the lone wolf is no longer alone then perhaps the courageous revolt was a mere facade. Utopian idealists lose their credibility when they join the established order. Hippies becoming yuppies? An entire generation becomes a farce. Lone wolves, heroes, rebels, and martyrs need to bleed profusely for their cause. Like Prometheus they must be chained, spiked to a cliff, and then abandoned to their torment. Only then will their tragic suffering attract genuine belief.

Ficke's drama nevertheless depicts the life of a lone rebel to be far superior to that of a sheepish slave. Autonomy, freedom of spirit, independence of will are extolled. Yielding, bowing down, complacency are debased. Man will no longer be man if he ever gives up or gives in.

>I am that dreamer to whose mounting dreams
>No bounds are set, no region which my will
>May not reach out toward. And I will create—
>I, and the souls that after me shall come—
>By passion of desire a pillar of flame
>Above the wastes of life.[36]

---

35. Arthur Davidson Ficke, *Mr. Faust* (New York: Frank Shay, 1922), p. 52.
36. *Ibid.*, p. 61.

Rubens, Peter Paul. *Prometheus Bound*. 1611-1612.

Chapter 3
Prometheus: A Sacrificial God

Before Faust and Satan, spiritual revolutions took place in the legendary realm of the Greek gods. Foremost of the rebels was a Titan, Prometheus, an elder god of the ruling order before the gods of Olympus. Prometheus stands above all mythological heroes as a Christ-like savior. Through his suffering and torment mankind was redeemed.

There are many variations of the Prometheus myth, but the story line is generally the same. Zeus, the ruler of the Olympian gods, finds fault with mankind and intends to destroy humanity by withholding fire. He will then create a new race of more subservient slaves. Prometheus, who loves mankind, intervenes and vexes the supreme god by stealing fire and giving it to man. Humanity survives and flourishes, learning the power of the arts and sciences (Prometheus, according to some, is the "tenth muse").

With fire as an ally, man is no longer vulnerable. Zeus is enraged by the treachery of Prometheus and has him bound to a cliff at the edge of the world. Each day an eagle from Zeus arrives to feed upon his liver, but Prometheus, being a Titan, is immortal and cannot die. His liver regenerates only to be eaten again the next day. His agony is therefore eternal.

The altruism Prometheus displays is doubly heroic because he knows beforehand what his fate will be. He has the gift of prophecy which he inherited from his mother, Earth (a Titan herself). His name means literally "foreknower."

Prometheus loves mankind, and for the sake of man he has defied Olympus and rebelled against the cosmic order. He sacrifices himself willingly, undergoing humiliation and torture. Prometheus is the savior of man, just as is Christ. He endures his suffering so that man may be redeemed.

Originally, however, Prometheus was treated humorously and in a lighthearted vein. His punishment, though severe, was seen as his due, a result of disobedience and tampering with divine decree. He was viewed as a malcontent and treated with disrespect. According to C.J. Herington:

> So far as we now know, Prometheus was felt by the Greeks generally --and even, to some extent, by Hesiod himself—as semi-comic: an impudent wag who tempted Providence in unusually ingenious ways, and was properly put down for it.[37]

It wasn't until Aeschylus wrote *Prometheus Bound* in the fifth century B.C. that Prometheus was given the legendary status of a tragic hero. Aeschylus was the first to extol the virtues of Prometheus. While still posed in the role of an arrogant braggart, Prometheus nevertheless acquires many positive traits. He complains about his fate in an ungodly manner (nobility and tragic heroes are expected to suffer in silence). And yet, he still suffers all the same—and he is suffering because he cared for man.

With *Prometheus Bound* Aeschylus endows the fire-giver with the altruistic role of a sacrificed savior. Despite the disdain of men or of gods, Prometheus resolutely stands above all.

> The *Prometheus Bound* of Aeschylus ends with the hero vanishing from sight amid thunder and lightning. It is assumed that the play was one of three, but its companions are lost.[38]

The second of the trilogy was *Prometheus Unbound* which purportedly dealt with the release of the suffering hero. Inspired by the legend of Prometheus, the romantic poet Percy Shelly wrote his own version of the lost drama over two millennia after the original.

The *Prometheus Unbound* of Shelly is tinged with a humanistic

---

37. Aeschylus, *Prometheus Bound* (London: Oxford University Press, 1975), p. 5.
38. Denis Donoghue, *Thieves of Fire* (London: Faber & Faber Limited, 1973), p.33.

Christian outlook. Prometheus loved mankind. He sacrificed himself for humanity. Shelly keys onto this altruistic theme of brotherly love and uses it as the resolution of the tragedy.

In a somewhat utopian, idealistic vision, Jupiter (Zeus) is overthrown by the primal spirit, Demogorgon. Judgment is pronounced and the tyrant sinks powerless into the abyss. Prometheus, after three thousand years of torment, is finally liberated by Hercules, the most courageous of all men. Mankind and the world itself are transformed. Universal love, truth, happiness and justice prevail.

The latter part of the nineteenth century brings a more modest, more godly Prometheus to light. The English poet Robert Bridges exploits the original gift of fire as the focus for his epic drama.

In *Prometheus: the Firegiver*, Prometheus is seen as the greatest of all gods. In the opening scene he appears on earth in the guise of a shepherd. Prometheus speaks to King Inachus as a prophet of fire. His role, through most of the drama, is to convince Inachus of the folly of appealing to Zeus for salvation, for it is Zeus who wants to destroy man by withholding fire. Inachus argues that perhaps it is punishment for their sins, that now that they repent by making sacrifices perhaps things will change. But Prometheus warns: "All is not good for man that seems god's will."[39] The gods are for themselves and what is best for them. Man is considered last, if at all.

Prometheus is shown contending with Zeus over the fate of man. He wants to save humanity and reside on earth.

> I would inhabit here and leave high heaven:
> So much I love it and its race of men,
> Even as he hates them, hates both them and me
> For loving what he hates, and would destroy me . . .
> For daring but to save what he would slay . . .[40]

Prometheus loves mankind. He sends man dreams and hope and inspiration. He wants man to prosper and fulfill his potential.

> But I, despised again, again upheld
> The weak, and pitying them sent sweet Hope,

---

39. Robert Bridges, *Prometheus the Firegiver* (London: George Bell and Sons, 1884), p. 21.
40. *Ibid.*, p. 4.

> Bearer of dreams . . . to cheer with visions fair
> Their unamending pains. . . .[41]

But, as this is not enough, Prometheus must blatantly defy the gods. Withholding fire ensures man's doom. And so Prometheus has stolen fire and brought it to Inachus, the wisest and kindest, as a gift to man. Inachus is finally convinced of the folly of his ways and accepts the words of Prometheus as truth. He even goes so far as to proclaim Prometheus greater than Zeus.

Prometheus knows fully what he has done. In a prophecy of his own future he foretells his fate.

> The woe of earth . . .
> That sight whose terrors shall assuage thy terror,
> Whose pain shall kill thy pain. Stretched on the rock,
> Naked to scorching sun, to pinching frost,
> To wind and storm and beaks of wingèd fiends
> From year to year he lies. . . .
>   —'tis thy tyrant's foe,
> Man's friend, who pays his chosen penalty.[42]

And thus Prometheus knows fully the consequences of his acts. He sacrifices himself so that man may survive—a Christ-like savior before Christ was even born. Prometheus is the ultimate redeemer, the bravest and most altruistic. For with foreknowledge he knows there is no escaping his doom. The Chorus appraises and bemoans the injustice of his lot.

> That he who loves thee and would aid thee, daring
> To raise an arm for thy deliverance,
> Must for his courage suffer worse than all?[43]

The altar is lit. Mankind has fire. Prometheus vanishes in a godlike ethereal manner without trace. The deed is done. It is irrevocable. All that is left is to await the Fates.

---

41. *Ibid.*, p. 6.
42. *Ibid.*, p. 52.
43. *Ibid.*, p. 55.

Various versions of the Promethean myth abound, specifically contradictory accounts of the fate of Prometheus. One version holds Prometheus forever upon the cliff with the eagle of Zeus feeding endlessly upon his liver. Another has Zeus demanding a prophecy of his own fate. When the prophecy is unfavorable, Zeus, in a raging fit, flings Prometheus into the abyss. Other versions have Prometheus giving Zeus the prophecy of who will be his successor. Prometheus is set free, having reconciled his differences with Zeus.

In another version the centaur, Chiron (himself a god) willingly takes the role of a surrogate sacrifice. The prophecy had been made that Prometheus would suffer until another god was willing to assume his suffering. Chiron is accidentally shot by the poisoned arrow of Hercules. He is immortal and thus must suffer eternally, but his misfortune may as well do someone good. He therefore offers himself in place of Prometheus. Zeus accepts the offer and liberates the Titan. Whether or not Prometheus gave Zeus his prophecy no one knows.

> One thing, however, is certain: in whatever way the two were reconciled, it was not Prometheus who yielded. His name has stood through all the centuries, from Greek days to our own, as that of the great rebel against injustice and the authority of power.[44]

But probably the most inspiring and satisfying version of the Promethean saga is that in which Hercules takes the leading role. This idealistic version shows that although Prometheus suffers, humanity does not forget. The strongest, most courageous of all men (actually half-man, half-god) sets forth to redeem the redeemer. Hercules defies the Olympian gods by shooting the eagle of Zeus with a bow and arrow. With the strength of a hundred men, he tears loose the shackles that bind Prometheus. The savior of man is himself saved and set free. And what is even more inspiring and satisfying is that this idealistic version of the Promethean myth springs from the idealism of mankind in general.

> One of the most persistent myths, that Hercules freed Prometheus from his unjust imprisonment and torture

---
44. Edith Hamilton, *Mythology* (Boston: Little, Brown and Company, 1942), p. 93.

by Zeus and became a god himself, rising to Olympus along with the Titan he saved, seems to have no specific individual source. It may be the one way that some wandering unknown poets and tellers of tales *wanted* the story to end. It gives them a kind of glory that many Greeks apparently felt both Hercules and Prometheus deserved as their final destiny.[45]

And so Hercules, the representative of man, shows that man, too, can have the divine attributes of gratitude, loyalty, self-sacrifice, and courage. At least one man, the strongest and best, will risk his own life to set the greatest Titan free.

---

45. Ellen Switzer, *Greek Myths: Gods, Heroes, and Monsters* (New York: Macmillan Publishing Company, 1988), p. 91.

To suffer woes which Hope thinks infinite;
To forgive wrongs darker than death or night;
   To defy Power, which seems omnipotent;
To love, and bear; to hope till Hope creates
From its own wreck the thing it contemplates:
   Neither to change, nor falter, nor repent;
This, like thy glory, Titan! is to be
Good, great and joyous, beautiful and free;
This is alone Life, Joy, Empire, and Victory![46]

Shelley

---

[46]. Percy Bysshe Shelley, *Prometheus Unbound* (from *The Complete Works of Percy Bysshe Shelley, Volume 2*) (London: Ernest Benn Limited, 1927), p. 262.

PART TWO

The Existential Revolt: Rebellion Against Life

CHAPTER 4. Vanity of Vanities: Misery and Absurdity in the World of Samuel Beckett

CHAPTER 5. The Tragedy of the Mouse: The Lonely Fate of an Existential Anti-Hero

CHAPTER 6. The Stranger: Prophet of Nihilism

CHAPTER 7. Nightmare Reality: The Heart of Darkness

Hopper, Edward. *Early Sunday Morning*. 1930.

"One sticks one's finger into the soil to tell by the smell in what land one is: I stick my finger into existence—it smells of nothing. Where am I? What is this thing called the world? . . . Who am I? How did I come into the world? Why was I not consulted . . . And if I am to be compelled to take part in it, where is the director? I should like to make a remark to him."[47]

            Kierkegaard

---

47. Sören Kierkegaard, *Repetition* (New York: Harper & Row, Publishers, Incorporated, 1941), p. 104.

INTRODUCTION

Of the three "revolutions," the Existential Revolt is the one most men experience. Why am I here? What was I created for? What is the meaning of Life? The answer is not forthcoming. May not even exist. And yet the existential rebel is prepared for any contingency. The question soon becomes, not "Why am I here?", but rather "Why do I wish to be here?" Not "What was I created for?", but rather "What do I wish to create?" And herein lies the problem. For the process takes time, the resolution needs maturity. But for the revolutionist this is no consolation. For the moment all he can do is prepare and wait.

For what? Godot?

Chapter Four deals with the absurdity of waiting for Godot. The meaning and purpose of life are not to be doled out on a silver platter. Beckett's view of life is shown to be metaphysically correct and genuine, and yet his characters and Weltanschauung are lacking in spirit and soul.

Chapter Five concerns Dostoyevsky's anti-hero, the Mouse. Still faced with the void, the "Wall," the unbreachable Structure, the Mouse nevertheless shows a certain courage, a spiteful dignity.

Chapter Six shows what happens when the waiting period is prolonged. When the gestation is alienated, the birth takes its nourishment from the void. Albert Camüs' Stranger becomes Nietzsche's "active nihilist" who destroys meaning, dragging man down into a spiritual abyss.

Chapter Seven presses the issue to the extreme. The madman Kurz is the pure embodiment of "the horror!" But Conrad shows the existential revolutionists a glimmer of hope. While Kurz is the natural outgrowth of a "disillusioned" encounter with the truth, the protagonist, Marlow, is the enlightened embodiment of the way—face the horror, but resist to your last dying breath.

The existential revolutionists of Part Two exemplify man revolted by the absurdity, madness, and horror of existence. They defy and rebel against the source of their frustration—even if it lies only in their imagination.

Chapter 4
Vanity of Vanities: Misery and Absurdity in the World of Samuel Beckett

"The end is in the beginning and yet you go on."[48]

Samuel Beckett, his writings, his characters portray the epitome of hopelessness and suffering, the human condition at its worst. The existential rebellion is not necessarily against God or some metaphysical order, but rather against the very conditions of existence itself. Man in the muck. Man in a random, senseless universe. The absurdity of life is the cause of the rebellion.

Indeed, Beckett's characters often crave some higher order. They call out in vain. For their own echo is their answer. It is a farce, a mockery, a senseless repetition. Their worst fear is that the higher order is only a delusion, that their one hope, their saving grace is only a symptom of their madness. And hence, their despair, their misery without end.

Beckett's power is in his ability to grasp the basic truth underlying every man's life: his aloneness, his uncertainty, his needs unfulfilled, his physical pain, and what's worse, his mental anguish. The basic truth is undeniable. Whatever good there is in life, there is also bad. People suffer. Innocent children die. Senseless accidents happen all the time. War, disease, starvation take their toll. Suffering is the rule, not the exception. As of 2018 UNICEF estimates that 8,493 children die every day from malnutrition. Happiness thus seems the exception

---

48. Samuel Beckett, *Endgame* (New York: Grove Press, Inc., 1958), p. 69.

for most people in the world.

It is for this reason that Beckett's writing, though depressing, rings true. Perhaps it is also the reason he was awarded the Nobel Prize for Literature in 1969. For people identify with the misery and suffering of his characters. The hopeless situations and tragic circumstances of his stories are their own.

Life is a roller coaster of ups and downs. Beckett examines minutely the downside. For him this is the basic constitution of life. The upside is a delusion so that the fall will be that much greater. Where everyone winds up in the end (if they're lucky) is to be forgotten, abandoned to old-age, disease and a miserable death. Life, for most people, is generally a letdown.

> Astride of a grave and a difficult birth. Down in the hole, lingeringly, the grave-digger puts on the forceps. We have time to grow old. The air is full of our cries.[49]

One sympathizes. One identifies. This is what life is all about. But is there nothing more? Nothing, at the moment. But for the future?—there is hope.

---

48. Samuel Beckett, *Waiting for Godot* (New York: Grove Press, Inc., 1954), p. 58.

Hope in Time
While Waiting for Godot
or
Salvation from the Muckheap

Waiting for Godot. The very title invokes time, anticipation, expectations. Waiting, hoping, dreaming, salvation—this is what differentiates man from animal. But it is also the cause of life's absurdity. For without a time-sense hope would not exist. And hope in a hopeless universe is the ultimate absurdity. The time-sense gives man hope, it allows him to endure. But it also make life that much more of a joke.

The problem is simple, though unresolvable. Hope requires time—a sense of the future. But the time-requirement allows people to suffer even more, for it prolongs the agony, makes the rejection and letdown even greater. It is the ultimate dilemma, the Catch-22. Hope helps us to endure the present, but it may also give us false expectations, thus making the future more unbearable. But hope is all we have. For the present is painful and miserable.

Would it then be better to extinguish hope? The answer Beckett gives is a paradoxical "NO!" His characters endure no matter what, no matter how much pain, boredom, frustration, or spiritual anguish. For hope is all that separates man from beast. It is the source of dreams and creativity. It is the wellspring of imagination and invention. If man gives up and relents to his condition, then he becomes little better than an animal.

Man must wait for Godot. There is nothing else he can do. For if he doesn't wait, then he must accept the present as it is. And the present, for most people, is unacceptable. It is only future possibilities that brighten man's life. To not wait for Godot is tantamount to killing oneself (at least as a man). Hence, Vladimir and Estragon's obsession with hanging themselves.

> Estragon: Didi.
> Vladimir: Yes.
> Estragon: I can't go on like this.
> Vladimir: That's what you think.
> Estragon: If we parted? That might be better for us.
> Vladimir: We'll hang ourselves tomorrow.
>   (Pause.) Unless Godot comes.
> Estragon: And if he comes?
> Vladimir: We'll be saved.[50]

Who is Godot? What is Godot? God? Salvation? The meaning of life? In the broadest sense Godot symbolizes hope. Not in himself per se. But rather in the effect he has upon those awaiting him. And for those not awaiting him? The effect is hopelessness and despair, a feeling that everything is meaningless. For those trapped in the present—hope no longer exists. They lose their sense of time. Past, present, and future all blend into one undifferentiated existence. There are no expectations, for everything is the same. In Act Two Pozzo illustrates how this lack of time-sense effects the perception of life's meaning.

> Pozzo: (*suddenly furious*). Have you not done tormenting
>   me with your accursed time! It's abominable!
>   When! When! One day, is that not enough for
>   you, one day he went dumb, one day I went blind,
>   one day we'll go deaf, one day we were born, one
>   day we shall die, the same day, the same second,
>   is that not enough for you? (*Calmer.*) They give
>   birth astride of a grave, the light gleams an instant,
>   then it's night once more.[51]

Hope fades without time. And in the present moment it vanishes altogether. Pozzo is hopeless and therefore helpless. He can no longer see. He must bargain with those who still have vision.

---

50. Beckett, *Waiting for Godot, op. cit.*, p. 60B.
51. *Ibid.*, p. 57B.

Vladimir is the sole character who maintains a time-sense. He is exasperated by the others who seemingly have no memory because they have no time. Godot's messenger-boy who claims never to have seen him before. Pozzo's transformation akin to a reincarnated life. And even Estragon himself who can't distinguish one day from the next.

Estragon's hope resides not in his time-sense, for he has none. Rather, it lies in the exact opposite; his timelessness—the world of his dreams. Estragon can escape the misery of the present by taking refuge each night in his dreams. As often as not they are nightmares, but they are nevertheless an escape, an alternative choice. And if they are terrifying enough, then perhaps the present, by comparison, won't seem so bad.

Vladimir, on the other hand, shuns the dream-world. It is fantasy. False hopes. It makes real life that much worse.

> *Estragon wakes with a start.*
> Estragon: (*restored to the horror of his situation*). I was asleep! (*Despairingly*). Why will you never let me sleep?
> Vladimir: I felt lonely.
> Estragon: I had a dream.
> Vladimir: Don't tell me!
> Estragon: I dreamt that--
> Vladimir: DON'T TELL ME!
> Estragon: (*gesture towards the universe*). This one is enough for you?[52]

Vladimir is pragmatic and wants no sugar-coating to his bitter pill. Life is bad enough without placebos complicating a possible cure.

But the panacea, does it exist? More than likely the answer is "NO!" It is the gloom and doom of Beckett's dead-end existentialism. His characters are generally trapped and suffocated by existence, hobbling along on crutches, crawling in the slime, forgotten, abandoned, blind, diseased.

> It will be the end and there I'll be . . . alone against the silence and . . . the stillness. . . . Moment upon moment, pattering down, like the millet grains of . . . that old

---

52. *Ibid.*, p. 11.

Greek, and all life long you wait for that to mount up to a life. Ah let's get it over![53]

And yet even in Beckett there is a sense of salvation after all. A glimmer of hope to the human condition. In the most metaphysical of his novels, *The Unnamable*, the nameless narrator rambles off in an endless conclusion:

> . . . you must say words, as long as there are any, until they find me, until they say me, strange pain, strange sin, you must go on, perhaps it's done already, perhaps they have said me already, perhaps they have carried me to the threshold of my story, before the door that opens on my story, that would surprise me, if it opens, it will be I, it will be the silence, where I am, I don't know, I'll never know, in the silence you don't know, you must go on, I can't go on, I'll go on.[54]

To continue. To say words. To narrate the story. To survive. Is that not enough? Is that not more than enough? What more Herculean task than to live without meaning? With only a vestige of hope? This is the paradoxical meaningful absurdity of Beckett's characters. To continue in spite of all odds, existential defiance in the face of the void—the abyss.

> Perhaps I could go on with my story, end it and begin another. Perhaps I could throw myself out on the floor. Dig my nails into the cracks and drag myself forward with my fingers.[55]

Beckett's characters, however despicable, still retain a certain dignity. They alone, are the witnesses, human consciousness of the absurdity. They never give up, no matter how much they complain. Prometheus himself could suffer no better. Indeed, they are the purest incarnation of suffering. Their identity, their meaning stems from

---

53. Beckett, *Endgame*, *op. cit.*, pp. 69-70.
54. Samuel Beckett, *The Unnamable* (from *Three Novels by Samuel Beckett*) (New York: Grove Press, Inc., 1958), p. 414.
55. Beckett, *Endgame*, *op. cit.*, p. 69.

their agony--their martyrdom.

> I say to myself—sometimes, Clov, you must learn to suffer better than that if you want them to weary of punishing you—one day. I say to myself—sometimes, Clov, you must be there better than that if you want them to let you go—one day. But I feel too old, and too far, to form new habits. Good, it'll never end, I'll never go.[56]

> Vladimir: Well? Shall we go?
> Estragon: Yes, let's go.
> *They do not move.*[57]

---

56. *Ibid.*, pp. 80-81.
57. Beckett, *Waiting for Godot, op. cit.*, p. 60B.

Chapter 5
The Tragedy of the Mouse: The Lonely Fate of an Existential Anti-Hero

In his story, "Notes from Underground," Dostoyevsky reveals the frustration and loneliness of an existential revolutionist. This Nietzschean rebel is bent upon pursuing the transcendental, the meaning and purpose of life, whether natural or preordained by God. But at the same time he is afraid that through fulfillment of this purpose, man will grow bored and stagnate. Does he therefore really want a purpose? This cynical nihilist consequently thumbs his nose at everything—his goal, his happiness, his own natural desires. He wants, and yet he doesn't want. He doesn't know what he wants—other than his freedom and individuality. He is torn between his natural longing for human companionship and his repugnance for such common herd instincts—his desire to transcend and reside solely in the rarefied atmosphere of "heightened consciousness," his spiritual loftiness (which is, in all practical purposes, his existential aloneness).

Eventually this man or mouse from underground opts for the metaphysical. Regardless of how disillusioned, frustrated and lonely he may feel, he attempts the impossible and remains true to his pursuit. His encounter with Liza signifies his last chance to become human. But he denies humanity and runs back to his mousehole of metaphysical defiance. His relationship with Liza ends in a sort of triumphant tragedy—triumph for his spiritual self and yet tragedy for his human self as well as for Liza.

The narrator, the anti-hero, readily compares himself to a mouse. A coward at heart, but nevertheless acutely aware of his surroundings with all its drawbacks and imminent dangers, the Mouse timidly ventures forth for a few morsels and then scurries back to his hole. He is a painfully self-conscious and incessantly reflective. He is a philosopher.

The Mouse, with its "heightened consciousness," refuses to believe man's behavior is controlled by the laws of science and nature. He denies this fatalistic belief while pounding his fists against against the stone wall of facts, facts which tend to indicate that man is a predictable animal. The Mouse refuses to accept the stone wall, for it seems to say that man is an automaton, that even the meaning and purpose of life is nothing but an equation.

The rest of humanity respect the wall and the limit it represents, then turn and walk away. The wall and life itself are not the challenge they are for the Mouse. "A wall has a calming effect upon them; it is as though it solved a moral issue—it is something final and, perhaps, even mystical."[58] The Mouse, however, never loses hope. He runs up against the wall, time after time, searching for a flaw, a weakness—a way to break through. Frustrated by the strength of the wall, he torments himself further with questions and doubts about his abilities, his shortcomings. And with other people laughing and spitting at the Mouse, he reaches a peak of humiliation and frustration. All he can do is run back to his mousehole or take another whack at the stone wall.

The Mouse reveals his open wounds to the reader. Going up against the wall, time after time, leaves you:

> . . . feeling that you've been short-changed, cheated, deceived, that everything is a mess in which it is impossible to tell what's what, but that despite this impossibility and deception, it still hurts you, and the less you can understand, the more it hurts.[59]

You envy the common man who, because of his ignorance, can still find happiness and peace of mind in the world. And yet you despise him, for he represents life without meaning or purpose. He is part of the masses, part of the herd.

As "twice two makes four," the Mouse believes man's purpose has also been logically arranged. If the stone wall could be breached, then

---

58. Fyodor Dostoyevsky, *Notes from Underground* (New York: The New American Library, 1961), p. 96.
59. *Ibid.*, p. 99.

all would be revealed. But at the same time he fears that man will stagnate should he succeed in penetrating the wall, for there would be no more challenge.

> And twice two, ladies and gentlemen, is no longer life but the beginning of death. At least, man has always feared this twice two makes four, and it's what I'm afraid of now.[60]

However, the Mouse also finds the "twice two" purpose a thing of beauty, even though he finds the "makes four" goal a thing of death. For he hates sitting with "arms folded" doing nothing in his mousehole. His dreams also show that the Mouse really loves the "twice two" purpose, for it fills him with hope, love, and happiness.

> . . . I had blind faith that, by some miracle, some force would push aside the confining screen, opening up a wide horizon, on which would be a worthwhile life work, useful and sublime, and above all, *all cut out and waiting for me* . . .[61]

The Mouse doesn't really want to be disagreeable. It's merely his way of asserting his freedom and individuality. He hates being predictable. He despises following the path of least resistance like everyone else. And thus his desires are contrary to what is natural.

His last chance to become natural, to become a human being and not a mouse, occurs when he meets Liza, a prostitute in a brothel. Almost as a joke, a playful act, he entreats and convinces her that she must lift herself from the gutter. She believes and follows him home, only to be symbolically slapped in the face. It was all fun and games. Had she really taken him seriously?

Deep inside, the Mouse wants to give and receive affection. His human side longs to be with Liza. He wants to be normal and happy, and yet it is also something he despises. He hates the human realm of rationalizations, weaknesses, and self-complacency. And so he acts mean and nasty simply to hide the feelings he can neither accept nor express. "I felt that they'd been swarming inside me all my life, trying

---

60. *Ibid.*, p. 117.
61. *Ibid.*, p. 136.

to break out, but I had refused to let them."[62]

Though paradoxically both admirable and despicable, the Mouse symbolizes the triumph of a "higher man" in Nietzsche's philosophy. For the Mouse poses a poignant question to the reader: ". . . what's better—cheap happiness or lofty suffering?"[63] Nietzsche answers Dostoyevsky and his Mouse by proclaiming:

> Surpass, ye higher men, the petty virtues, the petty policy, the sand-grain considerateness, the ant-hill trumpery, the pitiable comfortableness, the "happiness of the greatest number"--!
> And rather despair than submit yourselves. And verily, I love you, because ye know not today how to live, ye higher men! For thus do *ye* live—best![64]

Although the Mouse has triumphed spiritually, his human self despairs. Given a rare chance to regain his humanity, the Mouse rejects Liza and human happiness. "Never before had I gone through such anguish and remorse."[65] The Mouse is left endlessly frustrated by a stone wall he cannot break, humiliated by men who laugh and spit, tormented by a problem only gods can solve—left alone in a dark hole with no one to love, and no one who cares. One can easily imagine the life of the Mouse to be a tragedy, albeit a tragedy of his own making. And yet the Mouse says he may be more alive than anyone, for at least he faces reality while others escape into a dream-world where life's questions are easily forgotten.

> . . . all I did was carry to the limit what you haven't dared to push even halfway—taking your cowardice for reasonableness, thus making yourselves feel better. . . . We're stillborn, and for a long time we've been brought into the world by parents who are dead themselves; and we like it better and better.[66]

---

62. *Ibid.*, pp. 91-92.
63. *Ibid.*, p. 202.
64. Friedrich Nietzsche, *Thus Spake Zarathustra* from *The Philosophy of Nietzsche* (New York: Random House, Inc., 1927, 1954), pp. 321-322.
65. *Op. cit.*, Dostoyevsky, p. 202.
66. *Op. cit.*, Dostoyevsky, p. 203.

Hopper, Edward. *Nighthawks*. 1942.

Chapter 6
The Stranger: Prophet of Nihilism

"What I relate is the history of the next two centuries. I describe what is coming, what can no longer come differently: *the advent of nihilism.*"[67]

—Nietzsche

In his novel, *The Stranger*, Nobel Laureate Albert Camüs captures the existential defiance of one man's plight within a meaningless universe. Emerging from the ruins of the second world war, Camüs' first novel exemplifies the absurdity of life—a life where death is a ubiquitous shadow lurking in the background, where meaning and purpose are simply human constructions—sham delusions protecting us from the hopelessness of existence, and where all actions and interrelations are random and insignificant.

Camüs' existential premise is that man is lost within a world not of his making. He is simply thrust into an absurd universe where nothing really matters, a universe where life is inconsequential since it all ends in death. But even if man were immortal it would make little difference, for life itself has no purpose beyond the simple injunction: to live. Faced with this subtle emptiness, this valueless abyss, society contrives myriad systems of belief, countless avenues of escape from the impinging anarchy and chaos.

Only those strong enough to embrace the abyss are capable of rejecting traditional values and morals. This nihilism often ends

---

67. Friedrich Nietzsche, *The Will to Power* (New York: Random House, Inc., 1967), p. 3.

in suicide, but in cases of extreme indifference where even suicide requires too much effort, the result is the emergence of a tragic anti-hero—a "Stranger" alienated from mankind and from life. The anti-hero serves as a harbinger of death, a messenger and representative of the darkest abyss, a mirror reflection of the helplessness of man's soul. He appears as a sort of "Anti-Christ," an "inhuman monster" whose very existence exposes the games and illusions. He is the quintessential embodiment of existentialism—a paradoxical hero whose salvation lies within the joyful embrace of nihilism. Such is the metaphysical plot of Albert Camüs' novel, *The Stranger*. And such is the nihilistic syndrome currently plaguing modern life.

The plot of *The Stranger* revolves around a central character, Meursault, whose recognition of life's absurdity results in a careless indifference to societal values. Indeed, Meursault avoids any standards. His few innate values are not artificially acquired, but rather basic, instinctive drives such as the pleasures of swimming, sexual intimacy, or even the simple enjoyment of a tablet of chocolate eaten leisurely on a Sunday afternoon.

Meursault is existential to the core. He has no idea why he is here, or what he is doing, but simply proceeds with the mundane routine of life, because, at the moment, there is nothing better to do. However, Meursault differs from the rest of society in that he is strong enough to accept the inanity of life, rather than rationalizing it with a false system of transcendental "truth."

It is this false ideology that Meursault's very presence challenges and threatens to destroy. And it is for this reason, and this reason alone, that Meursault is executed. It is not because of the murder, for as he realized long before even committing the act: the murder itself is insignificant. "One might fire, or not fire—and it would come to absolutely the same thing."[68] Nor is he condemned, as many critics claim, simply because he failed to cry at his mother's funeral, so showing himself to be an inhuman "brute" defying sacrosanct social mores. The real reason for Meursault's condemnation is that he represents the truth behind the facade. Through his attitude, Meursault expresses the senseless absurdity, the "vanity of vanities," the underlying nihilism. He reflects the futility, the void, the inevitable doom, the lingering helplessness permeating life. And this, society cannot accept. The radical dissident, the prophet of nihilism, must be

---

68. Albert Camüs, *The Stranger* (New York: Random House, Inc., 1946), p. 72.

excised before his malign influence can infect and infest civilization's moral fabric. In the final analysis, Meursault is condemned to death simply because he exposes the meaninglessness of life.

From the first page of the novel, Mersault's apathy is apparent: "Mother died today. Or, maybe, yesterday; I can't be sure."[69] The fact that his own mother has just died makes little difference to our anti-hero. And why should it matter? For why should he feel gratitude for being born into a void? Instead of love and sadness, Meursault feels calm indifference. "I could truthfully say I'd been quite fond of Mother—but really that didn't mean much."[70] Meursault loves his mother "just like everybody else," but in this indifferent world even love fails to initiate a response.

Meursault fails to cry at his mother's funeral, not because it would be hypocritical, nor because he refuses to play his role, but simply because he feels no sadness, and hence, has no reason to cry. While talking to his lawyer, Meursault is befuddled by society's need for emotional expression:

> He went on to ask if I had felt grief on that "sad occasion." . . .
> I answered that, of recent years, I'd rather lost the habit of noting my feelings, and hardly knew what to answer.[71]

And thus it is not a rebellion or a defiant rejection of society's codes of behavior, but simply an honest expression of Meursault's indifference. Meursault is no existential or nihilistic martyr. He is no anarchic rebel railing against the injustices of life, advocating the overthrow of existing ideologies. Meursault is simply himself, naturally passive, filled with such apathy that he feels it useless even to try justifying his beliefs. And thus he passes the ultimate test of sincerity, for even to his own position Meursault is inured, for nothing in the world, not even himself, is of any importance. And so this passive, unconcerned anti-hero is actually the purest embodiment of nihilism.

Meursault's passive acceptance rather than active resistance makes him the best living example of absurdity. On the other hand, should he actively protest the sham of life, such an attitude would itself be a non-sequitur which destroys the basic premise of futility and inaction.

---

69. *Ibid.*, p. 1.
70. *Ibid.*, p. 80.
71. *Ibid.*, pp. 79-80.

For such a stance would place truth and rebellion as a higher form of meaning, and thus invalidate the metaphysical premise.

But Meursault is unconsciously true to his beliefs and therefore does not actively oppose the world. He simply observes the lies, the deceptions, and the illusions, but in no way cooperates, nor partakes in such deceit. And thus even his girlfriend, Marie, is subject to the Stranger's painful honesty. When she asks if he loves her, Meursault replies, " . . . much as before, that her question meant nothing or next to nothing—but I supposed I didn't."[72] And yet he is willing to marry her if it gives her pleasure, for it really doesn't matter one way or another. If another girl he liked made a similar proposal, he would "naturally" accept, for marriage was not really a serious affair.

And so, Meursault's relationships are formed out of apathy. He uses and is used without consideration or complaint, but simply for the practicality of the given moment. Since everything is meaningless, why try making them last? One should simply accept what the transient relation has to offer, since resisting would invoke too much meaning and effort. And thus Meursault is incapable of any sincere relationship because he realizes that they are merely temporal distractions. He is unmoved by both friends and lovers, for with transience everything becomes ghostly and unreal.

> . . . he slapped me on the shoulder and said, "So now we're pals, ain't we?" . . . I didn't care one way or the other, but as he seemed so set on it, I nodded and said, "Yes."[73]

Society and human relationships appear so inane to Meursault that he feels it useless to become actively involved. To be sure, he does become involved, but only as a passive agent. He cannot muster the energy required to become an active determining agent, but simply drifts along allowing anything to happen. And thus he once again passes the supreme test of indifference, for our anti-hero feels it worthless even to engage his own interests.

Ironically, this loss of ego and lack of self-interest are the very reasons people are drawn to Meursault. On the other hand, this selflessness is also responsible for his lassitude. For by realizing the futility of human actions, Meursault opens himself to mundane drudgery. Nothing is worthwhile other than what is needed to get by

---

72. *Ibid.*, p. 52.
73. *Ibid.*, p. 41.

from day to day. And so Meursault shows no interest in transferring to a new job in Paris, for as he says, " . . . I was quite prepared to go; but really I didn't care much one way or the other. . . . one life was as good as another, and my present one suited me quite well."[74] Berated for lacking ambition, Meursault recalls that in his student days he had plenty of ambition, but " . . . I very soon realized all that was pretty futile."[75] Indeed, everything to our modern anti-hero is "pretty futile," and thus he follows the line of least resistance.

It must be remembered that this futility applies to Meursault himself, and so as a logical concomitant of Meursault's indifference, is the indifference of Meursault to himself. As a result of this logical consistency, Meursault is alienated from his own being, his inner world of emotions and feelings. He may in fact relate his subjective impressions, but they are almost always conveyed with an air of objective apathy. Indeed, many times he fails to notice his feelings, for even to himself these are trivial matters.

Meursault is so inured to life, and to himself, that even curiosity is stifled by ennui. And thus the Stranger is reduced to observational reticence where conversation is limited to the most necessary thoughts. Or, as Marie inquires, ' "Don't you want to know what I'm doing this evening?" I did want to know, but I hadn't thought of asking . . .'[76] Meursault cannot even express simple curiosity, for he realizes instinctively that such thoughts are inane. And so he passes through life keeping mostly to himself. Or as Meursault explains in his defense:

> He led off by remarking that I had the reputation of being a taciturn, rather self-centered person, and he'd like to know what I had to say to that. I answered:
> "Well, I rarely have anything much to say. So, naturally I keep my mouth shut."[77]

Does Meursault really have nothing much to say, or does his overriding indifference keep his petty interests in check? Apparently Meursault represents the ultimate philosophical triumph, for without reflecting, he lives his philosophical resolves.

Meursault's apathy extends not only through his social and

---

74. *Ibid.*, p. 52.
75. *Ibid.*, p. 52.
76. *Ibid.*, p.54.
77. *Ibid.*, p. 82.

personal world, but also into his basic instincts. Meursault seems completely unnatural, for he is emotionally dead to acts of brutality and malevolence. They simply <u>are</u>, and must noncommittally be accepted. It is for this reason that Meursault feels neither anger nor pity when Salamano beats his dog. Even Raymond, the unsavory pimp, remarks ' . . . that it was "a damned shame," and asked me if I wasn't disgusted by the way the old man served his dog. I answered: "No." '[78]

Even when the misery is that of human beings, Meursault still cannot respond, but simply watches in apathy. He can't even be troubled to call for help, much less intervene to stop the violence which would be so easy to end. It simply isn't worth the bother, for it would be fighting an endless battle, a hopeless battle which could never be won. Meursault therefore resigns himself to inaction:

> The woman was still screaming and Raymond still knocking her about. Marie said, wasn't it horrible! I didn't answer anything. Then she asked me to go fetch a policeman, but I told her I didn't like policemen.[79]

Meursault's indifference ranges from the inner world to the outer world, from the subjective to the objective, from the world of thoughts to the world of actions. As the quintessential embodiment of nihilism, he feels that traditional ideologies are worthless. Marriage is no longer a sacrosanct institution, and so he behaves towards it as he would towards any rationalized convention—with an air of indifference. Funerals are no longer grave ceremonies symbolizing respect for the deceased and for the fateful processes of life and death, but rather a childish mockery of man's inability to cope with a meaningless life and an equally meaningless death. Sensing this self-deluding absurdity, Meursault cannot help letting his fundamental apathy show through. Unwittingly, almost without regard or forethought, he smokes cigarettes, drinks cafè au lait, falls asleep during his vigil, and tops off his offenses by neglecting to pay his last respects to his mother's body.

Not only is Meursault insensitive to the ceremony of the funeral— this in itself would be understandable in our jaded culture—but Meursault is just basically indifferent. He simply feels no grief over his mother's death. During a period of expected mourning, he goes

---

78. *Ibid.*, p. 34.
79. *Ibid.*, p. 45.

swimming, watches a popular comedy film, and winds up the day by making love to Marie.

Although his disrespect could be justified as escapism from grief, with Meursault this is not the case. He is fully aware that his mother's death is imminent and simply a matter of time. Her physical death merely confirmed his expectation. In fact, the Stranger is alienated from society because of his philosophical prejudice: that everyone he meets is already dead! And for the same reason Meursault is also alienated from himself, for instinctively he too sees himself as one of the dead. The pointlessness of it all makes even Meursault take note:

> It occurred to me that somehow I'd got through another Sunday, that Mother now was buried, and tomorrow I'd be going back to work as usual. Really, nothing in my life had changed.[80]

Meursault realizes the absurdity of life and death, and unwittingly assumes the role of the Prophet of Nihilism. Unwillingly, almost unconsciously, he embodies futility. Meursault is an unelected representative who cannot refuse his position. He feels guilt and responsibility for the absurdity. Thus, when it erupts and disrupts the normal routine, he is disconcerted and embarrassed. On taking leave from work to attend his mother's funeral, he is apologetic and weakly disclaims: "Sorry, sir, but it's not my fault, you know."[81] Throughout the story he makes such strange defensive comments, as though paranoid that people are blaming him for life's tragedy. Speaking of Meursault's mother, the warden explains that ' " She had no private means and depended entirely on you." I had a feeling he was blaming me for something, and started to explain.'[82] Meursault is guilty for his very existence. And thus anything he does, anything he says, is enough to gain some form of censure from the world.

> She made no remark, though I thought she shrank away a little. I was just going to explain to her that it wasn't my fault, but I checked myself, as I remembered having said the same thing to my employer, and realizing then it

---

80. *Ibid.*, p. 30.
81. *Ibid.*, p. 1.
82. *Ibid.*, p. 3.

sounded rather foolish. Still, foolish or not, somehow one can't help feeling a bit guilty, I suppose.[83]

Meursault emerges from the abyss as the purest embodiment of existential nihilism. And as such, his every action and inaction manifest these heretical views. The Stranger's very existence threatens to undermine the established order—an order which society strives to preserve. And thus the Stranger and his opposing Weltanschauung must either be eradicated or suppressed. The turning point comes when the "Outsider," the "Stranger," becomes the ultimate manifestation of nihilism, and consequently also the ultimate threat. The logical development of Meursault's passive nihilism is its transformation into active nihilism. Mounting offense upon offense, he finally becomes the most abhorrent of all criminals, the murderer, the destroyer of meaning and life.

Throughout the story, Meursault has exhibited a passive and pessimistic outlook on life. Of course life is meaningless, but he nevertheless maintains an almost stoic endurance of his problems. On the other hand, in somewhat of an epicurean manner, the Stranger also follows the unconscious dictum that he may as well enjoy what little life has to offer, since tomorrow he not only *may* die, but most assuredly *will* die. It is for this reason that Meursault has no qualms about enjoying the sun and the sea, sexual intimacy, or even a bar of chocolate on a Sunday afternoon, for they are the only pleasures left to man. All other ideals, virtues, and morals are simply philosophical constructions to justify meaninglessness and death.

A joyful acceptance of transient pleasures is thus no contradiction of existential nihilism, for such a belief opposes only the fundamental illusion of meaning. Meursault does not grant the simple pleasures any meaning, but simply accepts them whenever and wherever they arise.

What happens during the murder is, however, a complete reversal of Meursault's natural behavior. He changes from complete passivity and indifference to violent activity and the supreme form of aggression. The psychological explanation is simple. Meursault begins to feel threatened, not just by the Arab, but by the environment, reality, and the world at large. "The glare of the morning sun hit me in the eyes like a clenched fist."[84]

---

83. *Ibid.*, p. 24.
84. *Ibid.*, p. 60.

Such statements of almost universal aggression abound throughout the story, mounting in intensity with the approach of the climactic murder.

> As I slowly walked toward the boulders at the end of the beach I could feel my temples swelling under the impact of the light. It pressed itself on me, trying to check my progress. And each time I felt a hot blast strike my forehead, I gritted my teeth, I clenched my fists in my trouser pockets and keyed up every nerve to fend off the sun and the dark befuddlement it was pouring into me. Whenever a blade of vivid light shot upward from a bit of shell or broken glass lying on the sand, my jaws set hard. I wasn't going to be beaten, and I walked steadily on.[85]

Meursault feels threatened by the world, completely overcome by its ever-growing hostility, a hostility which he perceives as an outright attack. The Stranger, hitherto allowed the freedom of passive indifference, suddenly finds himself being assaulted by the symbol of life—the sun. This threat issues not from the Arab, for he is only the scapegoat and not the instigator per se, but in reality the confrontation is between Meursault and the force of life.

> The heat was beginning to scorch my cheeks; beads of sweat were gathering in my eyebrows. It was just the same sort of heat as at my mother's funeral, and I had the same disagreeable sensations--especially in my forehead, where all the veins seemed to be bursting through the skin. I couldn't stand it any longer . . .[86]

All through life the Stranger has been a passive puppet and patsy. Pushed here and there, he accepted fate with apathy. However, now he finds himself the victim of an overtly hostile attack, and in one literally blinding moment of liberated frustration and rage, the Stranger fights back and pulls the trigger. This action in itself is insignificant, for Meursault is only reacting out of psychological self-defense. He is pressured into the act by the unexpected sensory attack

---

85. *Ibid.*, p. 73.
86. *Ibid.*, p. 75.

which assaults and threatens his existential reality.

> A shaft of light shot upward from the steel, and I felt as if a long, thin blade transfixed my forehead. . . . Beneath a veil of brine and tears my eyes were blinded; I was conscious only of the cymbals of the sun clashing on my skull, and, less distinctly, of the keen blade of light flashing up from the knife, scarring my eyelashes, and gouging into my eyeballs.
> Then everything began to reel before my eyes, a fiery gust came from the sea, while the sky cracked in two, from end to end, and a great sheet of flame poured down through the rift. Every nerve in my body was a steel spring, and my grip closed on the revolver. The trigger gave, and the smooth underbelly of the butt jogged my palm. And so, with that crisp, whipcrack sound, it all began.[87]

But it could have ended here! If Meursault had simply stopped after the first shot, or even continued firing in rapid succession, then all would be well, and the case could be considered merely over-reaction in self-defense with mitigating circumstances. The key point here, glossed over by most readers and by most superficial interpretations, is the momentary pause between the first and the succeeding shots. This is the key to understanding the theme and the turning point of the novel.

> I knew I'd shattered the balance of the day, the spacious calm of this beach on which I had been happy. But I fired four shots more into the inert body, on which they left no visible trace. And each successive shot was another loud, fateful rap on the door of my undoing.[88]

The Stranger could have stopped or simply have gone on firing in rapid succession, but after the first aggressive and protective shot of self-defense, he pauses, he reflects, he is fully conscious, if only for a moment, of the consequences of his actions. The inhuman Stranger "knows" and realizes the significance or insignificance of what he is about to do, and yet he proceeds to execute his nihilistic deed and

---
87. *Ibid.*, pp. 75-76.
88. *Ibid.*, p. 76.

begins pumping the prostrate body with extraneous shots. And this, and this alone, is the cause of his undoing. This is the decisive factor in assessing and proclaiming Meursault's guilt.

It makes no difference whether or not the Arab was already dead after the initial shot. Camüs is delinquent in providing clues to this paradoxically significant and yet insignificant matter. The reason is that it makes no difference one way or another. All that matters is the Stranger's motivating intention, and this is the basic theme of the novel. The rest, the so-called facts, are neither here nor there as far as the Stranger's philosophical metamorphosis is concerned. What happens during the murder is simply the logical extension of Meursault's apathy to the supreme form of nihilistic indifference to life. "One might fire, or not fire—and it would come to absolutely the same thing."[89]

And so the Stranger resumes his firing, not out of hatred or vengeance, but simply because it doesn't make any difference. Simply out of curiosity he goes on firing, wondering whether his actions will have any effect. "I fired four shots more into the inert body, on which they left no visible trace."[90] And so the Stranger's philosophical conviction has been experimentally confirmed: in the final analysis nothing one does makes the slightest difference, even discharging a gun into a human being ultimately leaves "no visible trace." This philosophical experiment is the cause of Meursault's undoing, for only an "inhuman monster" could carry out such a brutal act. The examining magistrate realizes the implications of the pause, and consequently is so shaken that he will not let go of this frightening aspect of the crime.

> "Why did you pause between the first and second shot?"
> ... I made no answer.
> During the silence that followed, the magistrate kept fidgeting, running his fingers through his hair, half rising, then sitting down again. Finally, planting his elbows on the desk, he bent toward me with a queer expression.
> "But why, *why*? did you go on firing at a prostrate man?"
> Again I found nothing to reply.
> The magistrate drew his hand across his forehead and repeated in a slightly different tone:

---

89. *Ibid.*, p. 72.
90. *Ibid.*, p. 76.

"I ask you '*Why?*' I insist on your telling me."
I still kept silent.[91]

What this episode signifies is Meursault's unconscious, philosophical metamorphosis which he himself does not yet recognize nor understand. Our modern-day anti-hero is actually innocent of the initial shot of self-defense, but guilty of the next four shots of nihilistic aggression. The Stranger resumes firing because it makes no difference, because *nothing* in reality makes any difference! With these four succeeding shots Meursault has transcended to the Nietzschean realm of "active nihilism":

> Nihilism. It is *ambiguous*:
> A. Nihilism as a sign of increased power of the spirit: as *active* nihilism.
> ... It can be a sign of strength: the spirit may have grown so strong that previous goals ("convictions," articles of faith) have become incommensurate ...
> It reaches its maximum of relative strength as a violent force of destruction—as active nihilism.
> B. Nihilism as decline and recession of the power of the spirit: as *passive* nihilism.
> ...The strength of the spirit may be worn out, exhausted, so that previous goals and values have become incommensurate and no longer are believed; so that the synthesis of values and goals (on which every strong culture rests) dissolves ...[92]

The Stranger has in fact become an active nihilist. Rejecting the weakness of "passive nihilism," he has transcended to the stronger realm of "active nihilism," and this is what society instinctively dreads. Meursault has nearly assumed his role as the Prophet of Nihilism—the first step in the evolution of Nietzsche's Superman. And this abominable annihilator of values society cannot accept, for the Superman and his precursor (the Higher Man) constitute the greatest threat—the destroyers of all traditional ideologies and meaning.

In the brief moment between the first and second shot, the Stranger has summed up and passed judgment on life—nothingness.

---

91. *Ibid.*, p. 84.
92. Nietzsche, *op. cit.*, pp. 17-18.

The examining magistrate fully understands the philosophical ramifications of Meursault's "pause," and thus he asks the Stranger whether or not he believes in God—the ultimate manifestation of society's belief in meaning. When Meursault says, "No," the magistrate collapses in his chair.

> That was unthinkable, he said; all men believe in God, even those who reject Him. Of this he was absolutely sure; if he ever came to doubt it, his life would lose all meaning. "Do you wish," he asked indignantly, "my life to have no meaning?"[93]

The Stranger cannot help but to render life meaningless, for his very existence, his every action and every thought exposes life for what it is—a petty sham. And hence Meursault is condemned, not because of an insignificant murder—such deaths occur by the thousands each day—but simply because he represents the meaninglessness of life, an emissary from the darkness of man's spiritual abyss.

If he had shown even the slightest remorse, the Stranger could have gained some form of pardon for his offense. But because he is indifferent to his crime, he is consequently served the harshest verdict possible: guilty of homicide *without* extenuating circumstances. By expressing remorse, our anti-hero would be admitting a mistake, a fatal error of judgment on his part. And thus Meursault could probably have saved his life, for by regretting his actions he would be acknowledging some form of meaning, some sense of purpose or direction from which he had strayed. And thus there would be a last vestige of hope, for his spirit and soul could still be redeemed.

The examining magistrate realizes the significance of remorse, for even if Meursault fails to subscribe to religion, even an atheist retains some measure of hope if he, at the very least, still values life. And so the magistrate poses his last penetrating question: does Meursault regret what he has done? "After thinking a bit, I said that what I felt was less regret than a kind of vexation . . ."[94]

And so Meursault's honesty seals his doom. By failing to regret his violent actions, or at the very least to express some kind of remorse, the Stranger is still reinforcing and reaffirming the murder, and thus

---

93. Camüs, *op. cit.*, p. 86.
94. Camüs, *op. cit.*, p. 87.

exemplifying the meaninglessness of life. The prosecuting attorney pounces upon this damning evidence, but the Stranger is either too dense or too indifferent to grasp its relevance.

> "And has he uttered a word of regret for his most odious crime? Not one word, gentlemen. Not once in the course of these proceedings did this man show the least contrition."
> ... I really couldn't understand why he harped on this point so much. Of course, I had to own that he was right; I didn't feel much regret for what I'd done.[95]

And thus the Stranger, the Outsider, the Prophet of Nihilism, has transcended morality and virtue. Having extended indifference to the highest degree, our anti-hero has passed into a metaphysical world "beyond good and evil." As the Nietzschean Higher Man, Meursault has surpassed the pettiness of mere humanity. The result is a disregard for all mankind, and a consequent loss in the Stranger's own humanity and soul.

> ... the Prosecutor was now considering what he called my "soul."
> He said he'd studied it closely—and had found a blank, "literally nothing, gentlemen of the jury." Really, he said, I had no soul, there was nothing human about me, not one of those moral qualities which normal men possess had any place in my mentality.[96]

And so, society revenges itself upon this most extreme iconoclast. In the name of the French people, Meursault is to be publicly decapitated for not believing in a meaning to life. He is to be executed, not because he committed a senseless murder, but because he is a soulless monster "devoid of the least spark of human feeling"[97]—an intransigent nihilist without hope of salvation.

In the end Meursault realizes his fate, but accepts it as part of his alienated destiny. The Stranger becomes the unbeknownst martyr for existential nihilism—"Mr. Antichrist," as the perceptive magistrate

---

95. Camüs, *op. cit.*, p. 126.
96. Camüs, *op. cit.*, p. 127.
97. Camüs, *op. cit.*, p. 129.

Metaphysical Rebellion

half-jokingly denotes. And thus the ironic circle is complete, for Meursault's fate is determined by "pure coincidence," his destiny determined simply as "a matter of pure chance." But the Stranger joyfully accepts his role as the Nietzschean Prophet of Nihilism. Overflowing with the spirit of active nihilism, he screams out and insults God's priest with profanity:

> ... it was better to burn than to disappear. I'd taken him by the neckband of his cassock, and, in a sort of ecstasy of joy and rage, I poured out on him all the thoughts that had been simmering in my brain.[98]

At long last Meursault is free from the chains of illusions which tie him to the world. Liberated from the tenacious bonds of hope, he is now certain about the world and about the utter futility of life—the vanity and hopelessness of human existence. As pure nihilism incarnate "all the time, I'd been waiting for this present moment, for that dawn, tomorrow's or another day's, which was to justify me. Nothing, nothing had the least importance...."[99] And so, the Stranger concludes his nihilistic diatribe with the darkest pronouncement ever made upon life:

> From the dark horizon of my future a sort of slow, persistent breeze had been blowing toward me, all my life long ... What difference could they make to me, the deaths of others, or a mother's love, or his God; or the way a man decides to live ... All alike would be condemned to die one day ... what difference could it make if, after being charged with murder, he were executed because he didn't weep at his mother's funeral, since it all came to the same thing in the end? The same thing for Salamano's wife and for Salamano's dog ...[100]

As for the symbolic Antichrist, the Stranger opens his heart to the "benign indifference of the universe," joyfully accepting his role as a martyr to the fatally fatalistic forces of universal Nihilism. All that remains to complete his success is for the world to fully acknowledge

---

98. Camüs, *op. cit.*, p. 151.
99. Camüs, *op. cit.*, pp. 151-152.
100. Camüs, *op. cit.*, p. 152.

him as the Prophet of Nihilism—the "Stranger" totally estranged from mankind and from life. "All that remained to hope was that on the day of my execution there should be a huge crowd of spectators and that they should greet me with howls of execration."[101]

And so in the end there is a strange form of salvation and dignity after all. From the dark emptiness of man's suffering, from the nihilism of man's spiritual abyss, arises a note of self-affirmation—a note of stoical resilience and defiance against life:

> ... The whole building was as quiet as the grave ... Then the dog began to moan ... and through the sleep-bound house the little plaintive sound rose slowly, like a flower growing out of the silence and the darkness....[102]

---

101. Camüs, *op. cit.*, p. 154.
102. Camüs, *op. cit.*, p. 42.

Fuseli, Henry. *The Nightmare*. 1790-1791.

Chapter 7
Nightmare Reality:
The Heart of Darkness

The last of the existential rebels, Conrad's hero, Marlow, shows an alternative course to Camüs' frustrated nihilism. The Rebellion need not take the form of hostilities or malevolence. It need not be "active" (in the Nietzschean sense) to be valid. What Conrad proposes is what Nietzsche might call "passive nihilism"—a renunciation, a Buddhistic denial. But, compared to Camüs' Stranger, Marlow embodies a maturity and wisdom that is far more profound and therefore convincing.

In Joseph Conrad's most popular short story, "Heart of Darkness," civilized life is viewed as a fictional device or facade hiding man from the nightmare of existence. (The story is true in the sense that it is based upon Conrad's real-life experience.) Modern life is hence tantamount to a dream, a fabrication designed to repress the animal nature of man, the darkness and horror lying latent within man's soul. Barbaric life, on the other hand, is an embodiment and glorification of this "horror." It is the quintessence of demonic madness and as such the only natural response. On the one hand is pure evil, on the other hand "silly dreams." Both are repugnant and so one is caught in a dilemma. The only solution, according to Conrad, is an acknowledgment of the "horror" (not an affirmation as with Kurtz) along with a stoic defiance of the festering evil—a Buddhistic acceptance and rejection, as it were.

This resolution, this acknowledgment builds slowly through a gradual realization, culminating with Marlow's all-encompassing lie at the end. Marlow—a man who despises lying and deceit—reaches his peak of conscious clarity by invoking a lie. It is a lie that summarizes the theme and philosophy of the story—that life is a dream, a work of fiction, a deception, that reality is a nightmare from which one cannot awaken. It thus makes no difference who believes what, for it is a dream. It is all a dream. It is a facade. It is a lie. But first, the "story" . . .

Marlow, the central character of the story, embarks upon a symbolic quest into the heart of the darkest continent in the world, the darkness within the heart of man's subconscious or soul, and the universal darkness within the heart of all life. From the beginning, hints of madness foreshadow the horror lying within. Marlow's predecessor, a former steamboat captain, was killed while sadistically beating upon a native chief. A misunderstanding leading to a quarrel resulted in a sudden explosion of anger, "so he went ashore and started to hammer the chief of the village with a stick. . . . he whacked the old nigger mercilessly . . ."[103] But what is unsettling is that this captain was "the gentlest, quietest creature that ever walked on two legs."[104] " 'The changes take place inside . . .' " explains the company doctor while measuring Marlow's head. " 'Ever any madness in your family?' "[105]

The madness is evident as the nightmare journey continues. A French ship is found senselessly shelling the coastline. Hidden enemies. Paranoia. "There was a touch of insanity in the proceeding . . ."[106] A feeling of enraged impotence pervades the air—a mindless violence aimed at everything and nothing. Further ahead Marlow comes upon the incessant blasting of the landscape for the construction of a railroad. However, "the cliff was not in the way or anything; but this objectless blasting was all the work going on."[107]

The warning is clear. There is a senseless violence lying in store at the center of the darkness. Marlow could turn back at any time, but a compulsive drive draws him on toward the abominable truth. It is Marlow's own repressed mania which is pulling him into the blackness of his soul. A "sense of vague and oppressive wonder grew upon me. It was like a weary pilgrimage amongst hints for nightmares."[108] Thus

---

103. Joseph Conrad, *Heart of Darkness* (New York: W.W. Norton & Company, Inc., 1963), p. 9.
104. *Ibid.*, p. 9.
105. *Ibid.*, p. 11.
106. *Ibid.*, p. 14.
107. *Ibid.*, p. 16.
108. *Ibid.*, p. 14.

Marlow and his predecessors are analogous to pilgrims journeying to their place of worship—the heart of darkness ruled by the demonic madman Kurtz. But the inward journey for most is simply too much to bear. The spiritual transformation is by nature necessarily for the worse, for it destroys one's illusions and reveals the decadence of one's soul.

> 'I wonder what becomes of that kind when it goes up-country? . . . The other day I took up a man who hanged himself on the road. . . . 'Hanged himself! Why, in God's name?' I cried. He kept on looking out watchfully. 'Who knows? The sun too much for him, or the country perhaps.'[109]

The country. An "implacable force brooding over an inscrutable intention."[110] It was not merely unconsciously violent, but rather actively malevolent, as though nurturing and preparing some evil vengeance. It lived. It breathed. It watched and waited. It was the hidden blackness of the universe reflecting the shadowy nature of man. And this vision, this revelation was enough to drive one insane. "We penetrated deeper and deeper into the heart of darkness."[111] Marlow and his "pilgrims" move further toward a nightmare confrontation with reality, their own souls mirrored in the image of a rational maniac, a man who embodies and delights in the horror of life.

Marlow follows upon the path of this demon named Kurtz and begins to glimpse and understand his own barbaric self. During the journey inward he witnesses the maddened frenzy of the natives. It was not that they were inhuman, but rather the very fact that they *were* human which was frightening and yet paradoxically thrilling. It was ugly, and yet it was nevertheless the truth. The savagery of Marlow's vision has struck a subconscious chord and rung true.

Marlow realizes that man's view of reality is delusion and self-deception. It is a sham created to hide the horrible nature of the world, of the universe, of every living creature including and especially man himself. Strangely enough, Kurtz himself was originally party to the mass-delusion. He was formerly an idealist who planned to enlighten the world, or at least the dark portions which instead enlightened or

---

109. *Ibid.*, p. 15.
110. *Ibid.*, p. 34.
111. *Ibid.*, p. 35.

rather darkened him.

> 'Men looked up to him—his goodness shone in every act.'[112] 'He drew men towards him by what was best in them.'[113]

Kurtz was the emissary of humanity in its attempt to civilize a barbarous world. He was writing a report and guideline for the "International Society for the Suppression of Savage Customs." In it he spoke in "burning noble words"[114] of the immense good that could be done in helping these primitive people. However he ends his report (after his corrupt transformation) with the clear and simple words: "Exterminate all the brutes!"[115]

Kurtz has been driven mad by his confrontation with the darkness, his spiritual and psychological descent into the quintessential evil of man's soul. However it is a madness of reality and not of delusion. Kurtz is insane because the universe is insane. It is a nightmare through which only sadistic madmen can survive, and a nightmare to which one must surrender one's soul—"how many powers of darkness claimed him for their own."[116]

Kurtz is adored by the natives who worship him as a god. This humanistic idealist is found taking part in "unspeakable rites," murdering ruthlessly, ransacking the countryside out of greed for more ivory. A fellow adventurer, the closest thing Kurtz has to a friend, was forced to surrender his ivory out of fear for his life.

> He declared he would shoot me unless I gave him the ivory and then cleared out of the country, because he could do so, and had a fancy for it, and there was nothing on earth to prevent him killing whom he jolly well pleased.[117]

Marlow comes face to face with society's false premises and illusions. Civilization is structured upon a foundation of lies—lies that would dissolve before the darkness of the truth, "rags that would fly

---

112. *Ibid.*, p. 78.
113. *Ibid.*, p. 77.
114. *Ibid.*, p. 51.
115. *Ibid.*, p. 51.
116. *Ibid.*, p. 49.
117. *Ibid.*, p. 57.

off at the first good shake."[118] There was no idealism here. There was no benevolence or humanism. There was only ruthless exploitation. Kurtz was only guilty of pressing the methods to the extreme. But everyone was doing the same. It was only a matter of degree. The attempt to civilize the barbarians was only a rationalization for the parlor-room conversation of women. It was all a game and a sham. All that mattered, all that ever mattered, was the lust for wealth and power inherent in man's soul.

The ivory trickled out as the "barbarian" culture was squeezed dry. The natives began starving, were forced into slavery, were humiliated and beaten. And this in the name of civilized humanity. Rather—inhumanity! But after all, what really mattered was that smooth, white ivory for billiard balls and piano keys. Ivory-tower "idealism"—the phrase carries a double-edge. The idealism was in fact the idealization of the ivory. And Kurtz was the head priest not just of the native savages, but of the "white" savages, the "pilgrims" and the Company who admired him for his powers—the dark powers that "had patted him on the head, and, behold, it was like a ball—an ivory ball . . ."[119] Kurtz had been transformed into the pure incarnation of his dream, a dream that has become a nightmare from which he can never awaken. Kurtz reigns supreme in both civilized and barbarian cultures, for they are, after all, simply two sides of the same madness.

Thus Marlow understands that humanity has gone astray, that it is laboring under a delusion in order to hide its animalistic intent. There is no underlying goodness either in man or in the universe. For it is a lie, a foolish lie. "Humanity" and its liars are content "to dream their insignificant and silly dreams."[120] Whereas the reality of the universe and the truth of man's being lies solely within the darkness of liberated animalistic instincts. Senseless murder, wanton depravity, sadism, torture, lust and greed—all are the exclusive province of the ultimate Absolute. At the heart of reality, whether conscious or subconscious, is the decadent madness of pure horror and evil. During a brief moment of lucidity as Kurtz lies dying, his last words of judgment as he cries out "at some image, at some vision . . . 'The horror! The horror!' "[121]

Mankind is hence left passively to accept its foreordained fate. And yet, what else can anyone possibly do? Should we, as does Kurtz,

---

118. *Ibid.*, p. 37.
119. *Ibid.*, p. 49.
120. *Ibid.*, p. 72.
121. *Ibid.*, p. 71.

not only recognize and surrender to the underlying horror, but actually affirm it, embrace it, and make it a part of ourselves? If this demonic force is in fact behind all existence, then would it not be best to simply accept it and live it through to the end? Should we not, as does Kurtz, become the ultimate embodiment of such evil—a representative and exemplar of the madness of life. Or should we, as does Conrad's hero, Marlow, acknowledge the truth of the horrible nature of reality, and yet resist it until our last dying breath—with the ascetic discipline of stoic defiance, with the stolid hardness and chilling wisdom of a Prometheus Unbound.

> Let the fool gape and shudder—the man knows, and can look on without a wink. . . . He must meet that truth with his own true stuff—with his own inborn strength. Principles won't do. Acquisitions, clothes, pretty rags—rags that would fly off at the first good shake.[122]

Marlow realizes the insubstantial, dream-like nature of conventional reality, and tries to warn others of the malevolence lying within the heart of the universe, the heart of darkness within one's soul. But as Marlow himself takes note of the perplexing predicament, "It seems to me I am trying to tell you a dream . . ."[123] All his attempts to convey a warning are apparently in vain, for man is a separate and isolated dreamer, an ivory-tower idealist oblivious to the truth. Or as Marlow soon realizes, "No, it is impossible . . . We live, as we dream—alone. . . ."[124]

In the climactic scene with Kurtz's "intended," Marlow finally realizes that it makes no difference. Dream. Reality. It is all the same. Truth has no meaning in a universe of lies. The idealist truth-seeker becomes an outright liar—in order to hide the truth?—in order to hide the nightmare at the core? "The horror! The horror!"

> " 'His last word—to live with,' she insisted. 'Don't you understand . . .'
> " 'The last word he pronounced was—your name.' "[125]

---

122. *Ibid.*, p. 37.
123. *Ibid.*, p. 27.
124. *Ibid.*, p. 28.
125. *Ibid.*, p. 79.

And so it is resolved. Marlow, with an almost Buddhistic understanding of life, realizes that human existence is tantamount to a lie. It is merely a matter of preference: dreams or nightmares. It is a frightful dilemma that can drive one insane. "It was written I should be loyal to the nightmare of my choice."[126] And so too is everyone free to choose. Kurtz's intended can remain with her silly little dream. Humanity can hide behind its silly little lies. It is a relative facade which makes no difference, for the paradoxical truth is that everything is a nightmarish lie, the only resolution being either madness or withdrawal.

Conrad ends his "Heart of Darkness" with a profound vision of human tragedy. Marlow—a man who by all rights should have been driven mad, one who peered over the edge of man's spiritual abyss—returns with only the bleak vision of utter darkness and horror. And so this sojourner and vagabond of the spirit, remains somewhat outside and aloof from human life—a cold, stern judge who knows the somber gravity of the truth.

> Marlow ceased, and sat apart, indistinct and silent, in the pose of a meditating Buddha. Nobody moved for a time. . . . The offing was barred by a black bank of clouds, and the tranquil waterway leading to the uttermost ends of the earth flowed somber under an overcast sky—seemed to lead into the heart of an immense darkness.[127]

---

126. Ibid., pp. 65-66.
127. Ibid., p. 79.

PART THREE

The Metaphysical Revolt: Rebellion for Autonomy*

CHAPTER 8. The Dream of Life: Kafka and the Quest for Reality

CHAPTER 9. Transcendental Nihilism: Life as a Creative Illusion

CHAPTER 10. The Philosophy of Superman: Evolutionary Existentialism

CHAPTER 11. The Outsider: Revolution of Meaning

CHAPTER 12. Cosmic Laughter: The Transcendental Game of Life

CHAPTER 13. Threshold: Evolutionary Conciousness

---

* Autonomy: "the quality or state of being independent, free, and self-directing . . ."[128]

128. *Webster's Third New International Dictionary* (Springfield, Massachusetts: G.&C. Merriam Company, 1961), p. 148.

" . . . I hear you say 'Why?' Always 'Why?' You see things; and you say 'Why?' But I dream things that never were; and I say 'Why not?' "[129]

(The Serpent exhorting Eve in the Garden of Eden)

George Bernard Shaw

---

129. George Bernard Shaw, *Back to Methuselah* (New York: Brentano's, 1921), p. 6.

INTRODUCTION

The final liberation: man as causa sui—first cause, the creator of his own soul. The metaphysical rebels of Part Three are engaged in the ultimate revolution. It matters not who did what to whom or when or why. The question is now. The answer is forever. Whether God created man or whether it was all a freak accident. Whether a higher order exists or whether it's simply man in the muck. These various alternatives are moot, they make no difference. For all that matters is what man wishes to envision and create.

The Metaphysical Revolt: mind and spirit elevated to the highest degree. An evolutionary movement in that the rebellion is positive in nature, affirming a higher world of values that man himself creates. Such a heroic stance is the highest form of spiritual autonomy. Each man becomes his own arbiter. Each man becomes his own god. It is the ultimate in metaphysical defiance.

Chapter Eight reveals Kafka's "Dream of Life." While most known for his nightmares, Kafka did cherish an idealistic dream. Man can create what he wants of his life. That he so often finds his way into the nightmares of others does not invalidate the possibility of the dream.

Chapter Nine and Ten deal with Nietzsche's Superman philosophy. Nihilism, being the only valid basis of a metaphysics, Nietzsche builds upon the void through a transcendental nihilism. The resulting philosophy of the superman is for the elite, for the higher men, for the philosophers of the future. For only they are capable of incorporating it into their being.

Chapter Eleven concerns Colin Wilson's "New Existentialism," an "evolutionary existentialism." The Outsider rebels against the meaninglessness of life. With the power of creative imagination, "the Strength to Dream," he perceives and reinforces a side of reality hidden by the mundane.

Chapter Twelve delves into Hermann Hesse's Magic Theater of possibilities, a metaphysical playground where anything can come true. Life is shown as an on-going work of art. It is experimental, it can be molded. It is essentially a "real dream."

"Threshold," the conclusion, is really only the beginning. This final chapter sums up the Metaphysical Rebellion, leaving man on the edge, ready to take the necessary leap. Man is finally causa sui—the creator of his destiny. Man alone is responsible for shaping reality into a dream.

Chapter 8
The Dream of Life:
Kafka and the Quest for Reality

Franz Kafka, one of the greatest novelists of the twentieth century, was also a challenging metaphysician as well. Within his "Weltanschauung" Kafka viewed life as a dream—a baffling manifestation of some hidden reality, and yet a reality which man could never comprehend. This reality is masked by deceptions and illusions, or in other words, by the outward appearances of life. Kafka recognizes these appearances for what they are—a dream—and then strives to clarify the underlying reality. However, the unforeseen problem which continually arises, not only through Kafka's stories but also through the story of Kafka's life, is that knowledge of reality can never be attained—that all that can be known is one's own subjective world of experience or, in other words, one's own subjective dream.

Kafka's novels and stories, notorious for their dreamy oftentimes nightmarish quality, employ a dream-like, surrealistic technique to express man's alienation in the universe—a logically insane universe which he cannot understand. In Kafka's view, life is a strange sort of dream, so radically removed and dissociated from reality that all that man is left with are the images of a dream.

The Kafkaesque plots and themes are generally the same. The central character, the hero and representative of man, enters the story (of life?) as an interpreter of dreams. Baffled by the illogic and concrete unreality of the world, the hero is overcome by the forces which control his dream, his destiny, his life. The usual result of this frustration and anxiety is the development of two major themes and atmospheres to Kafka's stories.

The first basic thematic structure is one of active questioning, investigation, Sisyphean endurance and passive defiance—a refusal, not to acknowledge, but rather a refusal to submit to and accept the underlying authority which governs life. This refusal to humble oneself "Before the Law," to prostrate oneself before "The Castle" of life, necessarily entails a nagging disruption, a gadfly annoyance which threatens the mundane order. One who assumes such a Faustian role will be shunned by the community (whether human or dogdom), and thus be alienated and alone, a metaphysical outcast. And thus, the dog-philosopher in "Investigations of a Dog"[130] stands apart from the rest of his species. He cannot accept the lies and excuses with which his fellow canines are smugly content, but must instead rush here and there posing questions, conducting experiments, and in general threatening to undermine the peaceful world of established dogdom.

In a similar vein K., in *The Castle*,[131] feels himself to be alienated from the world of man (the village) and isolated from the structure of life (the Castle). But this is actually beneficial to K.'s purpose, for just as the investigator in "Investigations of a Dog" must find means such as fasting in order to dissociate himself from life (thus enabling him to remain aloof as the supreme, objective judge), so too does K. come to the Castle of life maintaining that he is the long-awaited "Land-Surveyor" who will observe and record the Castle's metaphysical landscape—the metaphysical structure of reality and life.

What no one realizes (perhaps not even K.) is that from the first day of arrival, K. has been fulfilling his role as the Castle-surveyor, summing up and passing judgment upon the nature of life. This is why the villagers feel an aversion towards K., not because he is foolish and ignorant, but on the contrary because he is the most astute observer. His presence serves as a reminder and guilty conscience, nettling the villagers who would rather remain asleep. K. is the alarm which awakens them, not to reality, for in the final analysis reality can never be known, but rather to that twilight state between sleep and waking in which the dreamer becomes suspicious of his dream. Naturally the sleeping villagers would like nothing more than to turn off the alarm, roll over, and return to their pleasant dreams. But K. will not be so easily shut off. No matter how many obstacles are placed in his

---

130. Franz Kafka, "Investigations of a Dog" (in *The Complete Stories*) (New York: Schocken Books Inc., 1971), pp. 278-316.
131. Franz Kafka, *The Castle* (New York: Alfred A. Knopf, Inc., 1954).

path, K., "That everlasting Land-Surveyor"[132], will persevere until he understands.

As a modern Faustian hero refusing to submit to Castle authority, but rather challenging it to his last dying breath, K. is the exemplar of man's search for truth. Obviously he cannot help but fail reaching his goal, for the reality he is in search of can never be known. And yet K. does succeed to a limited extent as a free agent, a philosopher, and a lover of truth. For despite all the devices distracting K. from his quest, he nevertheless continually refuses to submit—constantly tracking down answers in his attempt to awaken.

The challenging and defiant aspect of this first and best thematic structure is one, not of optimism, but rather simply of a positive nature. K. does succeed to some extent, not in his quest, but rather as an individual who refuses to passively accept, but instead presses forth invading the Structure of existence, opening doors in the middle of the night, awakening frightened dreamers who would rather be left asleep. And thus K. assumes the role of an alien invader, an iconoclast, a doubter, a disturbance which threatens the pretended dream-order. And slowly this realization dawns on K.: it is not he that should be fearful of the consequences of his actions (as the villagers continually warn him throughout the story), but rather the Castle and its officials along with villagers themselves. Or as K. almost gleefully exclaims after the Landlady cautions him about Klamm, one of the Castle's higher authorities:

> " . . . and so I am prepared to put up with my ignorance, evil consequences and all, for some time to come, so long as my strength holds out. But these consequences really affect nobody but myself, and that's why I simply can't understand your pleading. . . . So what are you afraid of? Surely you're not afraid—an ignorant man thinks everything possible"--here K. flung the door open—"surely you're not afraid for Klamm?"[133]

And so this first thematic structure of hopeful defiance brings K. no closer to the underlying reality, but it at least imbues him with a certain power and independence, a status which allows him a feeling of integrity and self-esteem. Or as Kafka tentatively ends *The Castle*

---
132. *Ibid.*, p. 28.
133. *Ibid.*, p. 73.

with the words of the dreaming Landlady—a dreamer who does not wish to be awakened to the realization that she is dreaming: " . . . you are either a fool or a child or a very wicked, dangerous person. Go, go away now!"[134]

The second basic thematic structure of Kafka's stories and novels is one of nightmarish pessimism devoid of all hope, or rather hope is allowed and even encouraged, but only so that the central character is that much more defeated and hopeless in the end. The major premise of these stories is that within the underlying reality exists a hostile force, if not consciously then at least effectively, inimical to man. Or as Kafka explained to Gustav Janouch: "The dream reveals the reality, which conception lags behind. That is the horror of life—the terror of art."[135]

Once again the central character, the hero and representative of man, enters the story of life as an interpreter of dreams. Baffled by the illogic and concrete unreality of the world, the hero is again overcome by the forces which control his dream, his destiny, his life. However, in this second thematic structure the result of the frustration and anxiety is the gradual metamorphosis of dreams into nightmares. One finds oneself compelled by strangely irresistible forces to commit suicide by leaping off a bridge; stripped of one's clothing and forced to lie naked beside a dying man with a wound filled with worms; and in the most bizarre instance unnatural dream forces have transformed one's body into a giant bug! These situations, though frightening in themselves, are not simply Kafkaesque examples of dreams turned into nightmares, but rather a somber reflection of Kafka's own perhaps demented or perhaps enlightened view of life. It is not enough for this modern Faust to posit an inimical force controlling man's inner world of dreams; he also goes so far as to presume that this force is determining man's destiny and life. For as Kafka explains, "The dream reveals the reality . . ." And thus he believes that the insanity of dreams is actually a reflection of the insanity of life. Whereas real life, on the other hand, is also conversely a concrete reflection of the world of dreams. The difficulty arise from the ambiguous terminology.

Kafka felt that human life was essentially unreal, simply as a result of its removal or dissociation from the primal source or from

---
134. *Ibid.*, p. 412.
135. Gustav Janouch, *Conversations with Kafka* (New York: New Directions Publishing Corporation, 1969), pp. 55-56.

the absolute reality. Everyday life and the normally presumed reality are therefore, in effect, actually a dream. Dreams, however, revealing the illusion of life, consequently maintain a greater semblance of the truth, and therefore are a more accurate portrayal of reality. Not the "absolute reality," but the only reality Kafka felt man could know—the elusive dream-world of existential reality. And it is obvious from Kafka's literary oeuvre that he began to suspect, and in the final analysis actually believed, that the "absolute" was in fact the existential dream unreality—that all man could know, that all that existed was the delusive madness of a paradoxically real nightmare.

And so, Kafka's view of life was at some times and in some sense that of a pessimistically paranoid and nightmarish world scheme. It must be stressed that this unsettling Weltanschauung is not simply a fictional device used for the express purpose of selling books. But rather it is the tragic world of frustration and paranoia through which the fragile Franz Kafka attempted to live his life. The absurdity of the situation is that whether ultimately true or false, it does not alter the fact that Kafka *suspected* his philosophy to be true. Whether in reality he was laboring under a delusion, or whether he was actually perceiving the truth, makes no difference. For such is the reality in which Kafka lived and died, such is the dream-nightmare of Kafka's own inner life.

In his most terrifying and also his most popular novel, *The Trial*, Kafka has his hero awaken "one fine morning" to find himself under arrest. He is never formally charged with a crime, but is nevertheless somehow already guilty from the start. All his attempts at a defense are frustrated and in vain, for he has no idea of the actual charge, and therefore cannot possibly ascertain either his innocence or his guilt. All his efforts to understand the "Law" are futile, for in the end, without a hearing or trial, the hero is evidently condemned to death. "On the evening before K.'s thirty-first birthday"[136] he is accosted by two "gentlemen," two "tenth-rate old actors," and taken forcibly to an abandoned quarry where he is stretched upon a boulder for execution.

> Then one of them opened his frock coat and out of a sheath that hung from a belt girt round his waistcoat drew a long, thin, double-edged butcher's knife, held it up, and tested the cutting edges in the moonlight. Once

---

136. Franz Kafka, *The Trial*, (New York: Alfred A. Knopf, Inc., 1956), p. 279.

more the odious courtesies began, the first handed the knife across K. to the second, who handed it across K. back again to the first.[137]

And so, with panic and a last desperate attempt at hope, K. wonders whether he will be saved in the end. Is there really a hidden meaning to it all? Is there a universal justice to life? Or is reality simply a nightmare of madness and evil.?

> Where was the Judge whom he had never seen? Where was the High Court, to which he had never penetrated? He raised his hands and spread out all his fingers.
> But the hands of one of the partners were already at K.'s throat, while the other thrust the knife deep into his heart and turned it there twice. With failing eyes K. could still see the two of them immediately before him, cheek leaning against cheek, watching the final act. "Like a dog!" he said; it was as if the shame of it must outlive him.[138]

And so the force controlling both dreams and life reveals itself for what it is: a murderous band of sadistic cutthroats, a nightmare horror inimical to man. It is interesting to note that what Kafka posited as the insidious nature of reality was actually vindicated through the living example of Kafka's own life. After many years of continual suffering he died from tuberculosis or consumption—a wasting away of living tissue, a deterioration which, in effect, literally consumed him alive. Fortunately Kafka died before the crisis which overtook his family. For almost as though in confirmation of his paranoid pessimism, all three of his sisters came to the same fate as Joseph K.—exterminated like rats in Nazi death-camps.

It would be simple to classify Kafka's philosophy along the lines of his two thematic structures, and thus Kafka would view life as a baffling dream which stronger Faustian natures attempt to understand, or else as a nightmare—the result of an active malevolence. This would be an easy enough classification if not for the hopeful ending to his last novel, *Amerika*. For after a lifetime of being victim to misfortune after

---
137. *Ibid.*, p. 285.
138. *Ibid.*, p. 286.

misfortune, Karl, the young hero of the story, has his dreams fulfilled as he finds sanctuary and belonging within the "Nature Theatre of Oklahoma." For the Nature Theatre is a mystical wonderland where every wish comes true. And this is the crux of the issue, for Kafka believed that life was a mysterious dream, a *real* dream admittedly, but a dream all the same. And when people have no idea of their true identity (as does Karl—the original title of *Amerika* was *The Missing One*) they can become trapped in the prison of another person's dream—a dream which can eventually transform into a nightmare. And this is the world within which Karl has lived most of his life.

But with the Nature Theatre, one can fashion one's destiny by creating one's own dream. Unlike his former life, Karl no longer need conform to preconceived notions of identity. If he wishes to call himself "Negro," then so shall it be. The officials of the Nature Theatre simply act as spiritual counselors and guides, showing Karl the way to his true identity or "self." They seem to know by divine intuition the Karl which will blossom forth as a dream. But this is not to say that the Nature Theatre is nothing more than Karl's dream. Nor is it, on the other hand, simply his vision of death. If there is any vision or dream involved in the plot, it is that of Kafka's own metaphysical dream of life. For there is a reality factor in the story which a simple dream-interpretation or a paradisiacal death-interpretation must either ignore or deny.

> "Well, you can't turn into an engineer all at once," he said, "but perhaps it would suit you for the time being to be attached to some minor technical work."
> "Certainly," said Karl. He was perfectly satisfied..."[139]

But what difference would all this make if it were simply a dream or a vision of death? How could it possibly matter if Karl assumed the role of actor, engineer, or technician? The answer is that Karl is definitely not dreaming, and he is obviously not dead. What is happening is that the Nature Theatre is a metaphysical realm taking place here and now. And as such it is intimately connected and interrelated with the "real world." Karl's duty is not simply to fantasize or dream his life away in some transcendental paradise, but rather to work and mold himself into an individual identity—to create a real dream out of the unreality of life.

---

139. Franz Kafka, *Amerika* (New York: Schocken Books Inc., 1954), p. 290.

Amerika is a unique expression, not necessarily of Kafka's belief in a benevolent cosmos, but rather simply of Kafka's hope and longing that somehow, somewhere, there really is indeed one. Or as I would interpret the major theme of the novel: we must create our own dreams and live them through to the end, rather than allowing dreams or nightmares to live through us. Such is the optimism behind the Nature Theatre of Oklahoma. For as Max Brod confirms:

> In enigmatic language Kafka used to hint smilingly, that within this "almost limitless" theatre his young hero was going to find again a profession, a stand-by, his freedom, even his old home and his parents, as if by some celestial witchery.[140]

And thus there is hope within Kafka's oeuvre. Life is a dream, but the dream is all we have. Only Kafka himself is awake, not to reality, but to the dream. Kafka is a dreamer who realizes he is dreaming, and yet no matter what he does he can never possibly awaken, for the reality he awakens to is itself only a dream. And thus he stands apart and above the mass of sleeping humanity, isolated and alienated from the world of human life. In his fragment "At Night" Kafka illustrates his dilemma poetically. "Deeply lost in the night.... All around people are asleep.... Why are you watching? Someone must watch, it is said. Someone must be there."[141]

---

140. Kafka, *Amerika, op. cit.*, p. 299.
141. Kafka, *The Complete Stories, op. cit.*, p. 436.

I have suddenly awoke in the midst of this dream, but merely to the consciousness that I just dream, and that I *must* dream on in order not to perish; just as the sleep-walker must dream on in order not to tumble down. What is it that is now "appearance" to me![142]

Nietzsche

---

142. Friedrich Nietzsche, *The Joyful Wisdom* (New York: The Macmillan Company, 1924), p. 88.

Bockland, Arnold. *Isle of the Dead*. 1883.

Chapter 9
Transcendental Nihilism: Life as a Creative Illusion

Kafka's dream/life approach in literature has its counterpart in modern philosophy. Friedrich Nietzsche saw life as a "creative illusion," an appearance, in essence—a playful dream. In Nietzsche's metaphysics "truth" per se does not exist. All man knows, can ever know, are varying perspectives on existence. Everything is relative and in continual flux. This rejection of absolutes, this denial of "objective reality," has led to Nietzsche's acceptance of himself as a nihilist. But is Nietzsche really a nihilist? And, if so, how can any life-affirming philosophy, such as Nietzsche's, take root in nihilism?

Nietzsche is *not* a nihilist. On the other hand perhaps he is, perhaps he is the "perfect nihilist"—so far beyond petty bourgeois nihilism that his nihilism has transcended. It has become ineffable. Such is the paradoxical nature of the problem, a Janus-faced, twofold contradictory dilemma. Nietzsche *is* a nihilist, but of a different kind—a nihilist who affirms at the same time that he negates. It is a childlike creative-destruction, a playful yes and no, a building-up of a sand castle which is then joyfully destroyed. Nietzsche *is* a nihilist, and yet he is also *not* a nihilist. He is a transcendental nihilist who has surpassed logical description.

Perhaps the best explanation of the paradox comes from Nietzsche's own words. In his preface to *The Will to Power* Nietzsche considers himself "as the first perfect nihilist of Europe who, however, has even now lived through the whole of nihilism, to the end, leaving it behind, outside himself."[143] Nietzsche has so fully experienced,

---

143. Friedrich Nietzsche, *The Will to Power* (New York: Random House, Inc., 1967), p. 3.

digested, and assimilated his nihilism that he has completed the process and excreted the harmful wastes. The vitalizing, nutritive elements of nihilism have been integrated into his being. The rest has been eliminated. Nihilism, per se, has been transcended.

But what is nihilism?

According to *The American Heritage Dictionary*, nihilism is a "systematic denial of the reality of experience and rejection of all value and meaning attributed to it."[144] Does Nietzsche reject the value and meaning of experience? Obviously not. Those familiar with his writings know that experience is one of the few things Nietzsche *does* value. In *The Genealogy of Morals* he ridicules "knowers" or philosophers for their abstract absorption in knowledge and mind. "As for the rest of life—so-called 'experience'—who among us is serious enough for that? Or has time enough?"[145]

Thus Nietzsche believes that experience *is* important. The problem is simply that the meaning and value of that "real life" experience has become warped by man. Religion, philosophy, society, and culture have resulted in a totally distorted vision of life. In this sense Nietzsche is indeed a nihilist, for he systematically attacks and invalidates all previous value assumptions. No philosopher has ever made such a thorough and penetrating argument against the credibility of such sacred institutions. Nietzsche proceeds ruthlessly to overturn all law-tables, undermining and toppling all "idols" of truth. Such is Nietzsche's own explanation of his work, *Twilight of the Idols: or How to Philosophize with a Hammer*: "to *sound out idols*. . . . to pose questions here with a *hammer* and perhaps to receive for answer that famous hollow sound which speaks of inflated bowels . . ."[146]

This is where Nietzsche is confused as a total nihilist and negator. He criticizes so thoroughly that nothing is left. He destroys all idols. He destroys all "truths." He sounds out all systems of values and beliefs and if it doesn't "ring true" (which they never do) they are smashed by his critical hammer and wit. It is not a matter of a denial and rejection of *all* values, but simply that of a rejection of all current values. Nietzsche does believe in values and meaning, but only those values and meaning which he himself creates. It is the basis of his

---

144. Peter Davies (editor), *The American Heritage Dictionary of the English Language* (New York: Dell Publishing Company, Inc., 1973), p. 477.
145. Friedrich Nietzsche, *The Birth of Tragedy and The Genealogy of Morals* (New York: Doubleday & Company, Inc., 1956), p. 149.
146. Friedrich Nietzsche, *Twilight of the Idols and The Anti-Christ* (Baltimore: Penguin Books Inc., 1968), p. 21.

philosophy of the superman. For the superman is himself a creator of values. He is the "Causa Sui"—the creator of his own soul, a legislator of his own reality and meaning.

Thus Nietzsche's superman philosophy is nihilistic only in relation to mankind or the herd. It is herd idols and ideology that Nietzsche wished to destroy. As far as the superman himself is concerned, meaning and value do exist. They are simply of a different order. They are internally generated, autonomous ideals. Hence Nietzsche's diatribe on all religions and gods, for to posit a transcendental meaning and order is anathema to "free spirits." To such spirits gods do not exist, "for what would there be to create if gods—existed!"[147]

But beyond this nihilistic rebellion for autonomy is a metaphysical rebellion—a nihilism of the spirit, a time when even one's own values lose meaning. According to Nietzsche, this "dark night of the soul" is a necessary requisite on the pathway to the superman. It is an essential step in confronting and liberating one's self. In *Thus Spoke Zarathustra* Nietzsche proclaims:

> What is the greatest thing you can experience? It is the hour of the great contempt. The hour in which even your happiness grows loathsome to you, and your reason and your virtue also.
> The hour when you say: 'What good is my happiness? It is poverty and dirt and a miserable ease.'[148]

Thus it is only after one's great denial, one's rejection of everything, that one is free to create. Otherwise one is hampered by bondage to old idols and obsolete meanings. Truth and meaning must first be destroyed before one can effectively create. Thus Nietzsche's nihilism acts as a spiritual catharsis, a metaphysical catalyst for furthering an evolution of consciousness. It is the nothingness and the abyss of Nietzsche's writings, an emptiness which must be surmounted in order to make one free. "Man is a rope, fastened between animal and Superman—a rope over an abyss.[149] The abyss is necessary, and yet this nihilistic void represents a great danger to those who must cross it, for "whoever fights monsters should see to it that in the process he

---

147. Friedrich Nietzsche, *Thus Spoke Zarathustra* (Baltimore: Penguin Books Ltd., 1969), p. III.
148. *Ibid.*, pp. 42-43.
149. *Ibid.*, p. 43.

does not become a monster. And when you look long into an abyss, the abyss also looks into you."¹⁵⁰

The spectacle is frightening—a labyrinthine emptiness which can be escaped from only by creating meaning, a void which can be filled only by inventing one's own substance. It can drive one insane. It is the ultimate test of the will to power. One can degenerate and become a monster. One can transcend and become a god. But how is transcendence possible when nothing is "real" or "true?"

TRUTH
The Ultimate Error

> There are many kinds of eyes. Even the sphinx has eyes—and consequently there are many kinds of "truths," and consequently there is no truth.¹⁵¹

"What are man's truths ultimately? Merely his *irrefutable* errors."¹⁵² According to Nietzsche, the idea of truth is itself an erroneous concept. Absolute truth, per se, does not exist. Rather, what man is faced with is a multitude of varying and contradictory perspectives each of which is as valid or as invalid as the other. The only difference is in their subjective effects. All is error. And yet all is true. Truth is perspectival. It is a relative opinion on the nature of existence. It varies. It is in flux.

> The world with which we are concerned is false, i.e., is not a fact but a fable and approximation on the basis of a meager sum of observations; it is "in flux," as something in a state of becoming, as a falsehood always changing but never getting near the truth: for—there is no "truth."¹⁵³

Man's "truths" are therefore not in themselves errors, for they are simply one way of viewing the world. The error Nietzsche speaks of is simply the attitude these perspectives assume when they become "irrefutable," when they become absolute. As long as these truths are considered only relative or perspectival they function as any viable

---
150. Friedrich Nietzsche, *Beyond Good and Evil* (New York: Random House, Inc., 1966), p. 89.
151. Nietzsche, *The Will to Power, op. cit*, p. 291..
152. Friedrich Nietzsche, *The Gay Science* (New York: Random House, Inc., 1974), p. 219.
153. Nietzsche, *The Will to Power, op. cit*., p. 330.

framework, but once they are irrefutable, once they are no longer questioned, that is when these truths become errors. An example is that of logic and scientific methodology. These frameworks are valid and productive. They work, and in Nietzsche's term "vitalize" to a certain degree. The problem occurs when logic and scientific reasoning work so well that they are no longer questioned as perspectives. They become idolized and sacred. They become absolute and thus stagnant. They become "TRUTHS." They become errors. "*What is truth?*—Inertia; that hypothesis which gives rise to contentment; smallest expenditure of spiritual force . . ."[154]

When considered as only relative frameworks, logic and scientific reasoning are valid approaches. But when considered as truths they quickly become errors. For one can see no further. One becomes myopic and diseased—pigeon-holed in a perspective from which one cannot escape. In Nietzsche's essay, "Truth and Falsity in an Ultramoral Sense," he expounds on the deadening effect of man's acceptance of "truth."

> What therefore is truth? . . . truths are illusions of which one has forgotten that they *are* illusions; worn-out metaphors which have become powerless to affect the senses; coins which have their obverse effaced and now are no longer of account as coins but merely as metal.[155]

In fact, Nietzsche considers the very concept of truth to be erroneous. There is no realm of metaphysical, objective truth. All that exists is the world of perspectives and illusions—the "apparent" world—and man can know no other. "The 'apparent' world is the only one: the 'real' world has only been lyingly added . . ."[156] It is the nothingness that has tagged Nietzsche with the attribute of "nihilist." But there is no reason for despair. For this metaphysical abyss is a necessary proving ground for the development of the Superman. In his last unfinished book, Nietzsche explains how the lack of "truth," of "reality," of any "absolutes," can lead to a strengthening, not a weakening, of man's spirit—an enhancement of his "Will to Power."

---

154. *Ibid.*, p. 291.
155. Friedrich Nietzsche, *The Philosophy of Nietzsche* (New York: The New American Library, Inc., 1965), p. 508.
156. Nietzsche, *Twilight of the Idols, op. cit.*, p. 36.

> What is a *belief*? How does it originate? Every belief is a considering-something-true.
>
> The most extreme form of nihilism would be the view that *every* belief, every considering-something-true, is necessarily false because there simply is no *true world*. Thus: a *perspectival appearance* whose origin lies in us (in so far as we continually *need* a narrower, abbreviated, simplified world).
>
> --That it is the measure of strength to what extent we can admit to ourselves, without perishing, the merely *apparent* character, the necessity of lies.
>
> To this extent, nihilism, as the denial of a truthful world, of being, might be *a divine way of thinking*."[157]

And so, faced with a morass of fluctuating perspectives and appearances, man is challenged by the nihilistic void. The only way to survive and flourish, according to Nietzsche, is to become an artistic creator. By filling the void with one's own substance, one's own "truth," one can transcend nihilism by becoming God. It is by treating the world as a work of art that man can metaphysically prevail. For the artist uses illusions to their best effect. What's true or false is of little concern. All that matters is the degree to which these attitudes vitalize and convey an effect. For "the criterion of truth resides in the enhancement of the feeling of power."[158] What is false or what is an illusion is hence just as real or valid as any other perspective.

In fact, Nietzsche believes in the necessity of lies and illusions. Since lies and illusions are all we have, they must be accepted. "For all of life is based on semblance, art, deception, points of view, and the necessity of perspectives and error."[159] Thus it is a matter of strength to what degree man can not only accept the lie, but actually affirm it, take delight and nourishment from its insubstantial nature.

> . . . there is only *one* world, and this is a false, cruel, contradictory, seductive, without meaning—A world thus constituted is the real world. *We have need of lies* in order to conquer this reality, this "truth," that is, in order to *live*—

---

157. Nietzsche, *The Will to Power, op. cit.*, pp. 14-15.
158. *Ibid.*, p. 290.
159. Friedrich Nietzsche, *The Birth of Tragedy and The Case of Wagner* (New York: Random House, Inc., 1967), p. 23.

That lies are necessary in order to live is itself part of the terrifying and questionable character of existence.[160]

Furthermore, to Nietzsche, what are clearly lies and illusions are more "truthful" than truth itself—because truth itself doesn't exist. What passes itself off as truth is debilitating and devitalizing compared to joyful illusions that playfully acknowledge their deceit and thus more closely approximate "reality" or truth.

> The will to appearance, to illusion, to deception, to becoming and change (to objectified deception) here counts as more profound, primeval, "metaphysical" than the will to truth, to reality . . .[161]

It is for this reason that Nietzsche says "that art is *worth more* than truth."[162] And it is for this reason that the Superman is an artistic creator.

> This faith in truth attains its ultimate conclusion in us— you know what it is: that if there is anything that is to be worshipped it is *appearance* that must be worshipped, that the lie—and *not* the truth—is divine![163]

Nietzsche is hence a nihilist, but of a different kind—a transcendental nihilist who has "transvaluated all values." His creative mythologies, his perspectival nature of reality, his denial of truth and acceptance of the lie, result in a Weltanschauung which rests literally upon nothing. It is a nothingness which Nietzsche sees as embracing all existence—a world "enclosed by 'nothingness' as by a boundary . . ."[164] Thus, in a sense, Nietzsche is a paradoxical nihilist—one who believes in quintessential nothingness and yet nevertheless affirms and creates.

---

160. Nietzsche, *The Will to Power*, *op. cit.*, p. 451.
161. *Ibid.*, p. 453.
162. *Ibid.*, p. 453.
163. *Ibid.*, p. 523.
164. *Ibid.*, p. 550.

Friedrich, Caspar David *Wanderer Above the Sea of Fog.* 1818.

Chapter 10
The Philosophy of the Superman: Evolutionary Existentialism

Within the history of philosophy one man stands alone as the originator of a new mode of thought—Friedrich Nietzsche, the herald of the "philosophy of the future," the Superman philosophy of metaphysical autonomy. Considered in the light of modern-day existentialism, Nietzsche's philosophy can be termed retroactively as evolutionary existentialism, a form far superior to its decadent outgrowths. What distinguishes Nietzsche from his philosophical heirs is not the classical problems of freedom, meaning, identity, and so on and so forth ad infinitum, but rather the initial distinction of basic attitude, attitude inherent even before the problem is met. In simpler terms, rather than despairing over the existential condition of man, Nietzsche's elite of higher men and Supermen want it; they seek it out; they function at their peak within a relativistic and ultimately valueless void, for only then, only in a metaphysical abyss can the Superman begin to create, or rather re-create the world, only from nothingness can something truly begin. Thus Nietzsche's higher men and Supermen are the forerunners of a new class of spiritual rebels, a class that can be designated the "evolutionary existentialists."

Evolutionary existentialism can best be understood as spiritual autonomy raised to the umpteenth degree. What it concerns is not the basic theme of alienation, meaninglessness, and the problem of existence, for these themes are common to all existential philosophies. Rather, what is stressed is the evolutionary aspect of Nietzsche's Superman philosophy—a calculated attempt at accelerated spiritual growth. In this sense the common "problems" of existentialism are no longer viewed as problems, but rather as metaphysical requisites for raising one's level of consciousness. For only through total freedom can one be responsible for one's life. Only through disillusionment can one forge a new world.

Based upon the existential premise of freedom, alienation, and individual subjectivity, Nietzsche proceeds with a daring experiment—a conscious attempt to transcend the human; an affirmation of nihilistic chaos in a defiant movement beyond; a movement into a realm where one becomes one's own god. The transition necessarily entails hardship and despair. And thus, the higher man constantly fights upward along the evolutionary path, confronting and overcoming every obstacle on the way. Only thus can he possibly attain the level of the gods. Only by being true to himself can he find the strength and spirit to transcend.

"Who are we, really?"[165]: a fundamental question of philosophy. And so, the "higher man" begins with Nietzsche's disturbing challenge, not the simple "Know thyself" of ancient Greece, but rather a questioning, self-doubting—"Who are we, *really*?" Of the many possible answers most are comfortable, but false. From the start, the higher man casts off the illusions of the "herd," plunging into the bitterness of unacceptable truths. The higher man is incapable of accepting complacent delusions and fantasies. For he is revolted by agreeing with "the many-too-many," "the all-too-human."

What do we really know? That we were born into a physical universe and abide by the same physical laws as do all other animals. That many of us will suffer and all of us shall die, and that death will probably share the same quality as our existence before birth—nothingness. That all talk of spirituality and a divine spark in man comforts us, but is it true? That we see no more purpose in our lives than we see in the lives of the animals we eat off our plates. Depressing? If man were as objective as this, nihilism and chaos would inundate the world.

But with constant exposure to religion and social mores independence of mind yields. We believe what we have always wished to believe. We accept what others wish us to accept. The fear of a meaningless existence has been allayed, or at least forgotten. "Suffering had been interpreted, the door to all suicidal nihilism slammed shut."[166] We can now rest assured that life does have meaning, that

---

165. Nietzsche, *The Birth of Tragedy and The Genealogy of Morals, op. cit.*, p. 149.
166. *Ibid.*, p. 298.

we are simply undergoing a test, that "the universe is unfolding as it should."[167] What we do each day is all that can be expected, for what more can anyone possibly do? And so we fool ourselves and never again question "why?" But the day may come when suffering is at its peak that the hidden question emerges. That is the day we shoot ourselves, thus proclaiming the truth of nihilism.

The Nietzschean elite, however, pursue this metaphysical "why?" to the very depths of despair, nihilism for them acting as a catharsis toward understanding and liberation. Thus the higher types confront the existential condition of man, are true to it, incorporate it into their Weltanschauung and make it part of their being. For them, man must be true to the earth, the secular "here and now," rather than to some obscure, possibly illusory, metaphysical "beyond."

To Nietzsche, man is man, a physical being in a physical universe. Man is similar to the animals, but man may be surpassed. "Man is a rope stretched between the animal and the Superman—a rope over an abyss."[168] Most humans stay close to the animal side for fear of falling into the abyss. Only the courageous question themselves. Only the higher man ventures forth over the abyss. Only he can surpass "the petty virtues, the petty policy, the sand-grain considerateness, the ant-hill trumpery, the pitiable comfortableness, the 'happiness of the greatest number' —!"[169] Yet only he is in danger of falling.

The fall may result from the dizzying height, the thinness of the air, the isolation, the hesitation, or perhaps from the most deadly—a glance into the void. For with the vision of metaphysical nothingness comes a paralyzing fear, a realization of the precariousness undermining existence. Or in more intellectual terms: if man is like the animals, without a creator god, then what is the purpose of life? Such questions lead ultimately into a metaphysical labyrinth, for without purpose why attempt anything at all? Or rather, why not just do anything? Which way should one turn? Is not everything permitted? Is not everything within one's grasp? What is there to differentiate? Such freedom is the first step across the abyss.

But the uncertainty arises. One realizes that values are in point of fact relative and unstable, that in reality one is dangling precariously without foundation, without "true" goal. To Nietzsche, however, the question of life's purpose or goal is in itself a sign of spiritual

---

167. Max Ehrmann, *Desiderata* (Los Angeles: Brooke House, 1954), p. 36.
168. Nietzsche, *Thus Spake Zarathustra, op. cit.*, p. 8.
169. *Ibid.*, pp. 321-322.

decadence, for the word "purpose" implies that something has already been willed. It is the herd that wants things to be willed for them. Like children, they must be told what to do. Like slaves, they must be ordered about. But the Superman is a creator. He is the one who wills. He does not wish to follow; he wishes only to lead. For him God does not exist, "for what would there be to create if gods—existed!"[170]

But what would there be *worth* creating? If there is no design or purpose to the universe then life is meaningless, for if absolute values do not exist then nihilism is all that remains. Nietzsche realized that the intellectual search for truth would eventually lead to nihilism, but unlike others he realized that nihilism may be surpassed. For there is another stage in evolutionary consciousness beyond the abyss, a stage where man has become the master of his destiny, where man is the "Causa Sui"—the creator of his soul. Nietzsche envisioned himself "as the first perfect nihilist of Europe who, however, has even now lived through the whole of nihilism, to the end, leaving it behind, outside himself."[171] What this evolutionary existentialist proclaims is that it is only the weak and cowardly who stagnate with nihilism. The strong create their own values and manage to function in a meaningless world by organizing and determining a small portion of the chaos, the smallest and most chaotic—that portion within oneself. The challenge is therefore within the unlimited possibilities, the unrealized potential, the danger, the madness, the chance of sudden victory or sudden death, horror or ecstasy without a moment's notice. Thus the higher men not only accept the metaphysical abyss, but actually want it, delight in it, are thrilled by the dangers of a possible "fall."

> Dance, oh! dance on all the edges,
> Wave-crests, cliffs and mountain ledges,
>   Ever finding dances new!
> Let our knowledge be our gladness,
> Let our art be sport and madness,
>   All that's joyful shall be true![172]

Like children they play games on the edge of the void, chasing and shoving, prepared at any moment to plummet to their deaths. Like

---

170. Nietzsche, *Thus Spoke Zarathustra*, op. cit., p. 111.
171. Nietzsche, *The Will to Power*, op. cit., p. 3.
172. Friedrich Nietzsche, *Joyful Wisdom* (New York: Frederick Ungar Publishing Company, 1960), p. 369.

clowns and tightrope-walkers they challenge one another, boldly venturing across the "rope" of man. This light-hearted madness develops one's spirit. This experimental game-playing enlivens one's will. But such existential affirmation is possible only for the strongest of spirits, or as Nietzsche said of Göethe, who "knows how to employ to his advantage what would destroy an average nature."[173] For make no mistake, the Supermen are playing for the highest possible stakes—one's soul, engaged as it were in the most dangerous of all games—the game of *real* life. For it is only with games and daring experiments that new evolutionary avenues can be reached. It is only by confronting nothingness that man's consciousness can advance.

> *I teach you the Superman.* Man is something that is to be surpassed. What have ye done to surpass man?
>
> All beings hitherto have created something beyond themselves: and ye want to be the ebb of that great tide, and would rather go back to the beast than surpass man?
>
> What is the ape to man? A laughing-stock, a thing of shame. And just the same shall man be to the Superman: a laughing-stock, a thing of shame.[174]

Thus this new awareness will engender a transformation of consciousness. And this consciousness must necessarily begin through a confrontation with oneself—through the absolute freedom within the unmolded soul. But the weak-willed cowards, the "herd" of humanity, are afraid of this confrontation, this existential unrest. They are content to live an animal existence while at the same time fooling themselves that they are somehow "higher." Thus as Nietzsche explains: "A doctrine is needed powerful enough to work as a breeding agent: strengthening the strong, paralyzing and destructive for the world-weary."[175] The doctrine is the affirmation of the abyss—total disillusionment with mankind. Self-deception is hence anathema to the Nietzschean elite, for delusions entail weakness and vulnerability to life. Nietzsche explains further that,

---

173. Friedrich Nietzsche, *Twilight of the Idols* (Baltimore, Maryland: Penguin Books Inc., 1969, 1971), p. 103.
174. Nietzsche, *Thus Spake Zarathustra, op. cit.*, p. 6.
175. Nietzsche, *The Will to Power, op. cit.*, p. 458.

> My philosophy brings the triumphant idea of which all other modes of thought will ultimately perish. It is the great cultivating idea: the races that cannot bear it stand condemned; those who find it the greatest benefit are chosen to rule.[176]

The Superman is hence this new race of Being—the iconoclasts, the nihilists, the destroyers of, not only illusions, but much more importantly—destroyers of self-delusions. Thus the Supermen reject all conventional value-structures, for such structures are built upon the herd standards of weakness and deception. The elite, however, delight in pushing themselves to the limits of self-analysis, penetrating to the very core of truth. The Supermen are "curious to a vice, investigators to the point of cruelty, with uninhibited fingers for the unfathomable, with teeth and stomachs for the most indigestible."[177] By exploring the depths, the Superman has a clear understanding of himself. Nothing remains unknown. He is aware at all times of his desires and his abilities, his goals and his powers. The subconscious has become conscious, for he refuses to allow the influence of anything his mind does not know thoroughly. The Superman is not faint-hearted, he can face any hidden truth no matter how wicked or distasteful. He does not hide from himself, rather, he strives at all times to know what he is and what he can become.

Such a man is "ready for every feat that requires a sense of acuteness and acute senses, ready for every venture, thanks to an excess of free will..."[178] The Superman demands more of himself. He constantly puts himself to the test, strengthening and sublimating his impulses, overcoming himself again and again.

> The noble human being honors himself as one who is powerful, also as one who has power over himself, who knows how to speak and be silent, who delights in being severe and hard with himself and respects all severity and hardness.[179]

In such a way, the Superman begins to create value and meaning.

---

176. *Ibid.*, p. 544.
177. Nietzsche, *Beyond Good and Evil, op. cit.*, p. 55.
178. *Ibid.*, p. 55.
179. *Ibid.*, p. 205.

He organizes a small world of his own, the god of such a world, dictator in that he maintains control over himself and over his situation. Paradoxical as it may seem, the Superman draws his power from the existential void, from the freedom of "nothingness" he acquires his strength. Or as Zarathustra explains, "It is not enough that lightning no longer does any harm. I do not wish to conduct it away: it shall learn to work for me."[180] Thus, the encounter with nihilism serves not the role of a depressant, but rather the role of a catalyst to higher levels of consciousness. For the Superman masters the void and employs its power creatively. He is in fact actually metamorphosing into a god—transforming himself from an "effect" into a "cause." Or as Nietzsche wrote of Göethe in one of his last books, *Twilight of the Idols*:

> He did not desert life, but placed himself at its center. He was not fainthearted, but took as much as possible upon himself, above himself, into himself. What he aimed at was wholeness; he fought against separating reason from sensuality, feeling, and will. He disciplined himself into wholeness, he created himself. He envisaged man as strong, highly civilized, graceful in every gesture, self-controlled, having respect for himself as a creature who might dare to afford the whole range and wealth of being natural, of being strong enough for such freedom, the man of tolerance, not from weakness, but from strength, because he knows how to use to his advantage what would destroy an average person. Such a mind, having attained real freedom, lives in the very center of all things with a joyful and confident acceptance of fate, lives in the faith that . . . in the wholeness of life everything is affirmed and redeemed. He no longer negates.[181]

But finally one knows only what one wants to know, listens only to what one wants to hear. Nietzsche's time will never come. Civilization will continue, man will pass through his days. It is hopeless to believe that someday there will be a society of Supermen, without petty problems, without petty wars. For the Superman philosophy exists

---

180. Friedrich Nietzsche, *Thus Spoke Zarathustra* (New York: The Viking Press, Inc., 1966), p. 289.
181. Friedrich Nietzsche, *Twilight of the Idols* (undetermined translation and reference).

only for the few. It is a philosophy, as Nietzsche realized, "for all and none." "In the end things must be as they are and have always been—the great things remain for the great, the abysses for the profound, the delicacies and thrills for the refined, and, to sum up shortly, everything rare for the rare."[182] For only the strongest can endure the self-reflecting abyss. Only the elite are capable of affirming the truth—the "horrible ecstasy" found at the summit of the soul. For only then, only at the top, can one gaze down confidently into the darkness of the void. Only when empty and frozen can one face the paralyzing truth, without the danger of unbalance, without danger of a "fall." The strength is needed and is thus incorporated into being. The truth is faced no matter how distasteful or true.

Evolutionary existentialism thus brings one to the crossroads of human evolution. One must decide here and now, for once and for all. Reality or illusion? Master or slave? The abyss or the flatland? The Superman or the ape? The decision will be one which will forge and seal one's fate. Let us then not be too hasty. "Let us consider this idea in its most terrifying form: existence, as it is, without meaning or goal, but inescapably recurrent, without a finale into nothingness. . . ."[183] The decision is hence a decision which will last forever. The meaning of life extending beyond the limits of death. The abyss opened up and made one with life.

> And do you know what "the world" is to me? Shall I show it to you in my mirror? This world: a monster of energy, without beginning, without end . . . enclosed by "nothingness" as by a boundary . . . a play of forces and waves of forces, at the same time one and many, increasing here and at the same time decreasing there; a sea of forces flowing and rushing together, eternally changing, eternally flooding back . . . my *Dionysian* world of the eternally self-creating, the eternally self- destroying, this mystery world of the twofold voluptuous delight, my "beyond good and evil," without goal, unless the joy of the circle is itself a goal; without will, unless a ring feels good

---

182. Friedrich Nietzsche, *Beyond Good and Evil* (in *The Philosophy of Nietzsche*) (New York: Random House, Inc., 1927, 1954), p. 428.
183. Friedrich Nietzsche, *The Will to Power* as translated by Erich Heller, *The Artist's Journey into the Interior and Other Essays* (New York: Vintage Books, 1968), p. 193.

will toward itself—do you want a *name* for this world? A *solution* for all its riddles? A *light* for you, too, you best-concealed, strongest, most intrepid, most midnightly men?—*This world is the will to power—and nothing besides!* And you yourselves are also this will to power—and nothing besides![184]

Come my friends, those who wish to take a risk, come closer to the edge and look down into your soul. See how "the abyss yawns for you," wishing to swallow you up and never let you go, never again to be seen. Come closer. Do not be afraid. You are alone, and you will be forever alone. But the lightning is here, the lightning that strikes out your path again and again through the labyrinthine chambers of your soul—to what? . . .

---

184. Nietzsche, *The Will to Power, op. cit.*, pp. 549-550.

"He's a romantic. He's not real inside either. He needs unreality to stop him from feeling an insect."
Glasp said softly:
"We all need something to lean on."
"But we shouldn't. If a man could kill all his illusions, he'd become a god."
"Or kill himself," Glasp said.
"No . . . He'd be strong enough to live. People die because they don't know what life is."
Glasp said:
"Who does?"
"I do sometimes. Just occasionally. And I spend all my time trying to regain the insight."
"And what was your insight like?"
"I . . . It was a feeling of acceptance. It happened once when I was on Hampstead Heath, looking down on London. I was thinking about all the lives and all the problems . . . and then suddenly I felt real. I saw other people's illusions, and my own illusions disappeared, and I felt real inside. I stopped wondering whether the world's ultimately good or evil. I felt that the world didn't matter a damn. What mattered was me, whether I saw it as good or evil. I suddenly felt as if I'd turned into a giant. I felt absurdly happy . . ."[185]

---

185. Colin Wilson, *Ritual in the Dark* (Boston: Houghton Mifflin Company, 1960), p. 347.

Chapter 11
The Outsider:
Revolution of Meaning

Colin Wilson carries on where Nietzsche left off. He extends Nietzsche's metaphysics and applies them to daily life. As such he is more practical. His philosophical premise is the existential. He sees man confronted by the void and his dilemma is: now what? Unlike Nietzsche's elite who can fend for themselves, Wilson addresses the specific problems of the existential man. The first problem he defines is the emergence of "the outsider."

Wilson burst upon the intellectual scene with the publication of his first book, *The Outsider*. From obscurity and alienation (his own feeling of being an outsider) he won overnight acceptance into the social order. Wilson wrote *The Outsider* while camped on Hampstead Heath, spending his days researching and writing in the British Museum. Ironically, with the publication of his book, he became an instant celebrity. One moment he was a social outcast, an outsider, a bum—the next moment he won national acclaim, admiration and respect. One wonders how Wilson would have developed had his book been rejected. Nevertheless, *The Outsider* was praised by critics. Wilson was considered a "boy genius," one of the elite.

Wilson's first book announces the existence of "the outsider"—a misfit and outcast unable to adjust to society. The outsider can be of many types: sexual, criminal, intellectual, artistic. But all have one common denominator: a rejection of societal values culminating in a frustration of wills and drives. Wilson defines the problem, explores examples of various types, and ends by encouraging the outsider to develop the power to withstand societal pressures, to determine his own values, to stand alone (if necessary) within a reality he creates. Failure is simply a matter of lack of courage, strength, or faith.

The emergence of the outsider against society is the beginning of a revolution of meaning. It signals the next phase of human evolution, a sign that mankind is ready for more. How man copes with this "outsider syndrome" is a measure of his depth and maturity.

> Behind man lies the abyss, nothingness; the Outsider knows this; it is his business to sink claws of iron into life, to grasp it tighter than the indifferent bourgeois, to build, to Will, in spite of the abyss.[186]

Faced with the abyss—the meaninglessness of life, the vapidness of society, the futility of human endeavor—the outsider copes in different ways. Just being an outsider is in itself a statement, a rebellion, but still it is not enough. Something more is needed to get through the day. The criminal outsider strikes out at society. Anything is permissible, even murder, for when nothing is of value then only one's pleasure and comfort are to gain. In a similar manner the sexual outsider takes his frustration and jaded sexuality to the extreme. Obsessions, higher intensity and frequency, perversions, sexual crimes. Wilson considers both the sexual and criminal outlets for the outsider to be invalid, for the sexual orgasm provides a tantalizing taste of life-affirmation but it cannot be sustained, besides which the behavior is controlling and addictive. The will to power and dominance of the criminal outsider also ends in a cul-de-sac, for nothing of value or meaning is created. It is merely a reversion to the primitive, the beast in the jungle.

Wilson proposes at least three valid avenues for the outsider and gives three examples. The physical outsider—the Russian dancer Vaslav Nijinski. The artistic outsider—Vincent van Gogh. And the intellectual outsider—Friedrich Nietzsche. These outlets for the creative drive can provide man with a valid method to create his own reality, a meaning to supplant the meaningless world of human life. The problem is that these outsiders often stand alone, isolated, and misunderstood. As a result, the pressure of their individuality may be too much to bear. All three examples, Nietzsche, Nijinski, and van Gogh went insane, and the latter killed himself.

The problem seems to be how to gain the power to face the void, to master oneself, to have the discipline and faith to sustain one's Weltanschauung, one's world-view. It is these practical problems of the existential condition that Wilson vows must be addressed.

---

186. Colin Wilson, *The Outsider* (Boston: Houghton Mifflin Company, 1956), p. 181.

The New Existentialism

After the metaphysical rebellion of the outsider, what then? After the spiritual coup de grâce what is left for man to do. He is free, but for what? He has destroyed man's illusions, but still finds himself in the void. It is from this point that Wilson's New Existentialism comes into play—a positive approach to life that he designates "Evolutionary Existentialism."

Evolutionary existentialism can best be understood as an affirmation of man's existential condition. Such a philosophy surpasses traditional European existentialism, for such "dead-end" existentialism is totally lethargic and resigned, accepting without question the foreordained limits of the known. The trick is to elevate the existential premise to a new level. For, according to Wilson:

> Existentialism, far from being a dead philosophy, is in fact the only modern philosophy with a long and clear road of development ahead of it. The true 'founder' of this new existentialism is Nietzsche, for it was he who announced the advent of a new optimism.[187]

As with Nietzsche, Colin Wilson delights in the existential condition. Freedom, responsibility for one's actions, the authority to create one's standards and morals, to create one's "meaning of life." These conditions are not only desirable, they are essential. Transcending the boundaries of the "possible," such a vitalistic existentialism reaches ultimately into the "impossible," revealing to man an entirely new dimension of life, affirming spiritual autonomy whether metaphysically imposed or freely chosen.

This new, evolutionary existentialism deviates from the commonly understood existentialism in its approach to life. It sees man's own subjective, inner values as being an intricate component of existence. Reality is not just out there to be seen and judged. Man creates reality by his own moods and perceptions. In effect, man projects the reality he perceives. Life is like a movie that man produces and perceives simultaneously. He is integral to the creative process. If man does nothing, takes a submissive or passive role as does the typical

---

187. Colin Wilson, *Introduction to the New Existentialism* (Boston: Houghton Mifflin Company, 1966), p. 95.

existential approach, then life will appear boring, bleak, depressing, or even a nightmarish hell. It is like staring at a blank screen and wondering why nothing seems interesting. Or what's worse, gazing entranced at someone else's production (perhaps a soap opera or even a horror film) which is inauthentic and debilitating. To complain bitterly is an easy excuse for not envisioning a reality of one's own.

Colin Wilson terms this failure of the European existentialist (e.g. Sartre, Camüs, and Heidegger) "the passive fallacy." No longer deluded by religion or societal values, they look at the world neutrally and wonder why it seems neutral. They don't realize that they themselves have to take on the job of being God. The old joke "that existentialists have their heads up their asses and wonder why it's dark" fitfully illuminates their predicament. For what is needed is vision. The existentialists must raise their line of sight, they must climb the mountain to see the vista, the new horizons and realms of possibility.

And this is exactly the approach of the "new evolutionary existentialists." Bleakness, boredom, depression. Whose fault is that? It is one's own. It is each man's responsibility to create a vitalized life. Man must take an active approach to reality. He cannot sit back and watch the world pass by, for if he does, all he will see is a blank screen. The void, the abyss will be yawning in his face.

But how does one take an active approach? Wilson believes this can best be done by developing one's inner powers: strengthening consciousness, creative expression, imaginative visualization. In the sixth and last book of his "Outsider Cycle," *Beyond the Outsider*, Wilson emphasizes the truism man has known intuitively all along. Mind, ideas, imagination are all-important. It is what separates man from beast and is the avenue for further evolution. Teilhard de Chardin terms this realm of meaning and human spirit the "noösphere"—the domain man inhabits when he is inspired and ennobled.

The problem is that the noösphere is intangible, it is a matter of faith, idealism, a matter of perspective. And when it clashes with the mundane, the practical everyday reality, it often loses.

> Man's consciousness is focused in a narrow beam on the present, and the life-energies respond to the challenges of the present. When the consciousness is disconnected from the present and turns inward, the energies sink; the world of concepts cannot provide the same stimulus as

the world of present reality. (This, of course, accounts for the high mortality rate among the nineteenth century romantics.)[188]

The world of the secular and practical holds too much sway over man's consciousness. Those with vision are considered ivory-tower idealists, impractical dreamers. But it is these very dreamers that have expanded man's horizons, given man a sense of being closer to the gods. Art, literature, music, drama—even science and technology owe their debt to the realm of theory and imagination. We know that the ideal, the inner vision, the intangible is what is most important in life. And yet when it conflicts with everyday reality it usually proves an unworthy opponent.

> Man must learn to disconnect his consciousness-- and therefore his life energies—from presentational immediacy, and discover how to expand or narrow the beam of consciousness at will. The problem is that the intellectual—or imaginative—stimulus is usually so much weaker than the stimulus of 'hard fact'. And yet there are certain departments in which the vital energies respond to imagination almost as readily as to reality—sex, for example. There is no reason why they should not be disciplined to respond to urgency of concepts in the same way. And here again, we face the problem of 'nihilism'. If the world is regarded as meaningless, then imagination is only a form of escape, and ideas can only be 'speculations', devoid of urgency. If the idea that man is 'condemned to meaning' is accepted, then ideas become ploughshares, cutting into the soil of the mind, attempting to establish man's direct relation to evolution as a living reality instead of an abstraction. Without powerful intellectual preoccupations—that is, without ideals—man is the victim of triviality . . .[189]

The problem is that man is weak-willed and myopic. He has become jaded and can't see reality in a new light. A toddler sees wonder

---

188. Colin Wilson, *Beyond the Outsider* (Boston: Houghton Mifflin Company, 1965), p. 156.
189. *Ibid.*, p.156.

and imagination everywhere and thus lives intensely. But man has grown bored. He has accepted the limitations defined by others and doesn't realize they are self-imposed. It is as though he has blinders on. Wilson uses the analogy of a horse in the city that needs blinders to keep him from being distraught by traffic. Modern man also wears blinders and wonders why he can't see. The task of the evolutionary existentialists is to remove man's blinders and thus provide him, for the first time since childhood, with the power to creatively intensify his life. One way this can be accomplished is by overcoming simple habit.

Necessary Doubt: Rebellion against Habit

What is wrong with normal consciousness? Primarily it is a matter of habituation. Wilson considers habit a double-edged sword. It is both good and bad. It allows man to master complex skills and retain them without effort: riding a bicycle, driving a car, typing without thinking of each and every key. But, on-the-other-hand, habit dulls the senses, weakens one's grasp on life. It is like walking down the same street day after day. One fails to notice the details, the meaning, the beauty. After making love to the same person year after year it is no longer as romantic and passionate, something essential is lost. One becomes jaded and takes things for granted. The "robot" has taken over and does our living for us.

This "robot" certainly makes life easier, but it has become too efficient. This machinery of consciousness keeps things running, but at the cost of vitalized living. As a result there is boredom and depression, a sense of meaninglessness and futility. Man no longer experiences life, so how can life be appreciated? Wilson believes that this boredom from habituation is why some people need to engage in dangerous sports. Mountain-climbing, sky-diving, anything that can break the spell of everyday consciousness. Even the routine two-week vacation is life-enhancing. For from the first day of the vacation the senses are engaged. One is "ready" to have fun. Each moment is lived with expectation and intensity.

According to Wilson, this habituation occurs not only in the senses and experiences, but penetrates through to the way one thinks, one's thoughts have become habits, one's consciousness is no longer free. But freedom, for some, is perhaps the last thing they need.

In his detective-thriller, *Necessary Doubt*, Wilson explores the paradox of the freedom-habituation dichotomy. In brief, the plot is the pursuit of a Nietzschean-superman-type character. Suspected of murdering old men for their money, Neumann is found instead to have created a drug (neuromysin) that unblocks habit patterns, leaving the mind energized and free. His only crime, if there is one, is in allowing these rich men to be guinea pigs and of accepting large sums of money to continue his research.

Even Neumann's pursuers become convinced of the drug's importance. For the effects of neuromysin are extraordinary. Consciousness is intensified, sharpened to precision fineness. The world is seen through the wondering eyes of a child, but with the adult intellect intact. The only problem is that neuromysin needs further refinement and research, for a deadly side effect stems from the freedom-habituation dichotomy.

Habits make life easier, more routine, but also more monotonous and depressing. Remove the "robot" consciousness and suddenly one becomes free, energized, more intense. One is no longer trapped in habitual consciousness. One has myriad choices of action and perception. But a choice—for what? The sudden freedom is deadly. The rich, old men see with crystal clarity the emptiness of their lives. They don't know what to do and so they choose suicide.

But Neumann claims that this is only the result of an undisciplined mind that cannot bear total freedom. What is necessary is an intensified will, a purpose that can guide one through "the dark night of the soul."

Neumann's pursuers agree, although they still have their reservations, their "necessary doubts." For the taste of freedom given by neuromysin leaves no doubt about its importance. They see themselves spearheading the evolution of human consciousness. Neumann may or may not be a ruthless exploiter, a con man of the highest order. But what he has discovered is certainly worth gambling one's moral scruples. In fact, the moral dilemma Wilson ends with reflects back on the title and the central freedom-habituation paradox. Any faith or creed must allow for a "necessary doubt." For it is only by questioning and doubting that man's integrity remains intact. Wholesale acceptance is tantamount to slavery and brainwashing. Paradoxically, this questioning and doubting keeps the faith or creed alive and intensified. It keeps man on his toes, makes him experience a hundred times over his belief or disbelief. It is an essential part of philosophical integrity, consciousness probing every aspect and every angle, never settling down quiescently, never forgoing its "necessary doubt."

The Human Potential

> *"But we all had a common feeling—that man is not big enough, that no man who has ever lived has achieved a fraction of the greatness of which man is capable."*[190]

Wilson synthesizes his outsider stance with evolutionary existentialism and the freedom-habituation philosophy, merging them with "the third force psychology of Maslow" and the human potential movement. The result is a positive, life-affirming philosophy. Man is primed for an evolutionary leap in consciousness. Hidden powers, unknown potentials lie waiting to be used. Now that he is free, man can choose his own path of development. He can consciously become a self-actualized human being.

What Maslow contributed to psychology was an optimistic view of human nature. Rather than studying sick and diseased minds, as do all previous psychotherapies, Maslow wanted to understand healthy and enlightened minds. The result was the discovery that mentally healthy people have far more of what he terms the "peak experience."

The peak experience is a sudden sense of well-being and life-affirmation, an intense feeling that all is right with the world. It is almost mystical in nature. Maslow found that successful, mentally-healthy and self-actualized individuals looked at life in a far more positive manner. And as a result, as would be expected, peak experiences were common.

Colin Wilson combines Maslow's observation with a phenomenological approach to existentialism. Perception and awareness are seen as intentional efforts. Man does not passively experience reality. To a large extent he creates it by his attitude and expectation. If one looks at the emptiness, the boredom and drudgery of existence (as do most existentialists) then that is exactly what one will see. Whereas, if one looks at life in a positive, mystical mode, then by that very openness and intention that is how reality will be perceived. It is like the child's view of the world, unencumbered by routine and boredom. Christmas morning. The first day of vacation. One's senses are open. One is ready to have fun.

---

190. Colin Wilson, *Necessary Doubt* (New York: Trident Press, 1964), p. 228.

Wilson's optimistic existentialism coins the term "Faculty X" for this ability to see the world with the freshness, the vividness and clarity of a child. According to Wilson, development of this faculty is the evolutionary goal of mankind, for with it man can attain the level of the gods. Without it man will not only stagnate, but regress. Human culture will suffer, for it is this faculty that gives life meaning, a visionary goal. Absence of Faculty X bogs man down in the trivial, the animal—the need for comfort and reassurance: physical, social, and sexual security. How much life is wasted in pursuit of these vulgar, petty goals? Or as T.S. Eliot asks, "Where is the Life we have lost in living?"[191]

The challenge is to intensify and broaden one's perception of reality. By pure effort of will one can develop powers of awareness that can sustain Faculty X—each peak experience reinforcing and enhancing a further positive experience—a permanent chain reaction that is the ecstasy of creative, mystical genius. It is a choice between the evolutionary spearhead and the masses who believe there is "nothing to be done,"[192] who believe that the mundane will always have the final word.

> But the careers of the Beethovens, the Van Goghs, the Dostoyevskys, give lie to this low-spirited view. They affirm that man can be greater than he realizes by launching himself into the sea of chaos. They affirm that by turning his back on 'worldly values', by summoning an apparently suicidal courage, man can achieve a new plane of the heroic, a further step towards the god-like. This is the lesson of the Outsiders—a lesson of deliberate loneliness and reaction against the values of the mass, a revolt against the mob-conditioned desire for security.[193]

Hermann Hesse's *Steppenwolf* is a prime example of the outsider trapped in the bourgeois, struggling from the narrowness of existential depression to the mystical affirmation of the Magic Theater, from futility and boredom to rapture and awe.

---

191. T.S. Eliot, "The Rock," in *The Waste Land and Other Poems* (New York: Harcourt, Brace & World, Inc., 1962), p. 81.
192. Beckett, *Waiting for Godot, op. cit.*, p. 7.
193. Colin Wilson, "Beyond the Outsider" in *Declaration* edited by Tom Maschler (London: MacGibbon & Kee, 1957), p. 36.

"You remember how I brought Georgi to see you one evening, and he told you about his most important idea? Do you remember what that idea was?"

Zweig shook his head.

"It was this: that he suspected that every human being who has ever lived has wasted his life completely. Do you remember that?"

"I think so."

Neumann shrugged. "I know—it sounds obvious. I often heard him say it, but it never struck me as very important. But after his death, his mother gave me his writings—all his papers—and he had begun to write an essay on the subject. And for the first time I understood what he meant." Neumann stared at Zweig for the first time, and spoke deliberately. "He meant that *if* all human life has contained a certain basic error, then the man who realized this would be *completely alone*. He could speak to no one. Other people could only confuse his certainty."[194]

---

194. Wilson, *Necessary Doubt, op. cit.*, pp. 261-262.

Chapter 12
Cosmic Laughter:
The Transcendental Game of Life

In Hermann Hesse's novel *Steppenwolf* the main character, Harry Haller, encounters the laughter of the Immortals, a sudden breakthrough of the cosmos into the mundane world of human life. After a harrowing descent into the nether regions of his soul, Haller finally realizes that the world is a playground of infinite mutability, an ever-changing tapestry of meaning and light. The laughter of the Immortals, which signals the end of the book, represents Harry's understanding of the purpose of existence, a positive affirmation and childlike game-playing, as it were. The laughter is the philosopher's stone and secret of transcendence.

Harry's problem is that he takes life too seriously. Rather than enjoying and affirming with lighthearted gaiety, he insists on mulling over the problem of existence. And yet he fails to come to terms with the nature of life. Neither does he come to terms with the nature of his own self. Thus he is trapped in the vacuum of an existential void.

To be sure, Haller has glimpses of the divine through Göethe and Mozart and the timeless realm of the Immortals. But his gravity constantly draws him down into the world of bourgeois meaninglessness. He cannot yet exist in the rarefied atmosphere of the eternal. His subsequent disillusionment results in a bleak and pessimistic Weltanschauung, a nihilistic restlessness and denial of the human spirit. Hence, the "Steppenwolf Syndrome."

Harry's lack of faith in the Immortals causes him to vacillate between the polarities of the divine and the animal, an oscillation which catches him in the middle-ground of the bourgeoisie. Rather than accepting with levity this superficial realm of contradictions,

Harry's seriousness drives him to the brink of suicidal despair. As the Steppenwolf, he is floundering in the tepidness of a bourgeois hell when his Jungian anima, Hermine, liberates the lone wolf by showing him how to have fun and to dance—to forget his troubles and to delight in the mere appearances of life. As Haller begins to understand, Pablo and the Magic Theatre show furthermore that everything in life is only apparent manifestations. Thus it is a universal game—a process, not a goal. The myriad doors and strange mirrors of the Magic Theatre, as well as the psychedelic concoctions of Pablo's drugs, reveal the comical transience and flux of so-called "reality." Life is *not* what it seems. The world is *not* how it appears. Haller can thus envision and play reality however he pleases, for Mozart and the Immortals demonstrate the method of seeing through the appearance, penetrating the masks and illusions with the visionary spectacles of humor.

This is the lesson which Harry promises to learn: that life is a game to be played and enjoyed. Rather than mulling over the rules, the contradictions and discrepancies, Haller must delight in spontaneity and childish simplicity, for only thus can he see beyond the distorted radio music of life—the earthly static behind which plays the Handelian concerto, the cosmic melody and harmony which is the essence of the eternal. Harry perceives and is saved. The way to transcendence is to cosmically laugh at the apparent absurdity and madness, the distortions and strident discords of human existence.

What Nobel laureate, Hermann Hesse, reveals in *Steppenwolf* is that life is ultimately analagous to a "Magic Theatre" or dream—a metaphysical playground where anything and everything can, if dreamed with sufficient laughter, eventually come true. Life is hence a joke with transcendence as the punch line. It is an infinitely subtle game played solely by Immortals.

> "I understood Mozart, and somewhere behind me I heard his ghastly laughter. I knew that all the hundred thousand pieces of life's game were in my pocket. A glimpse of its meaning had stirred my reason and I was determined to begin the game afresh. . . .
> One day I would be a better hand at the game. One day I would learn how to laugh. Pablo was waiting for me, and Mozart too."[195]

---

195. Hermann Hesse, *Steppenwolf* (New York: Holt, Rhinehart and Winston, 1957), p. 243.

Van Gogh, Vincent. *Starry Night*. 1889.

Chapter 13
Threshold: Evolutionary Consciousness

"You, too, have mysteries of your own. I know that you must have dreams that you don't tell me. I don't want to know them. But I can tell you: live those dreams, play with them, build altars to them. It is not yet the ideal but it points in the right direction. Whether you and I and a few others will renew the world someday remains to be seen. But within ourselves we must renew it each day, otherwise we just aren't serious."[196]

In his classic science-fiction movie, *2001: A Space Odyssey*, Stanley Kubrick ends with the image of a fetus floating freely against the background of space. The message: mankind has not yet been born. Not just that man, as a race, is in his childhood or even infancy. But that spiritually, to all intents and purposes, man has not even emerged from the womb. We are still developing, being nurtured, have yet to awaken our potential. We are priming ourselves for an entrance into reality. Visually the effect is stunning. Man's spiritual consciousness as prenatal. It explains a lot—why the world is so disoriented. Göethe expresses the same sentiments in literature by proclaiming: "Life is the childhood of our immortality."[197] Our everyday world that we take so seriously is only fun and games to gain experience, practice for maturity, merely a trial run. Life, according to Göethe, is only a prelude to something greater.

---

196. Hermann Hesse, *Demian* (New York: Harper & Row Publishers, Inc., 1965), p. 115.
197. Johann Wolfgang von Göethe, (unknown reference or attribution)

In a similar vein Arthur C. Clarke (the author of *2001: A Space Odyssey*) closes his book, *Childhood's End*, with advanced alien "Overlords" returning to earth to bear away the mutated children of mankind. They are the end-products, the fruit which the "Overmind" literally planted in "the beginning." All of humanity and human civilization were simply the means to a mysterious end, the manure through which this special race of children could gain nourishment, grow to maturity, and eventually blossom. These children are the fruit of millions of years of evolution. And the alien Overlords have finally come to reap their harvest.

It is an image paradoxically both melancholy and inspiring. Melancholy for the rest of humanity left with a feeling of "now what," the feeling of sadness after a lifelong goal has been attained, the aftermath, the afterbirth, the feeling that the party's over. But it is inspiring for those identifying with the children. Reality is awaiting them—not a mock, practice-world of the human. The aliens will show them realms where they were really meant to be. The children, the "real" humans will finally utilize all the potential held in store. They are, in effect, demigods who eventually merge and become one with the Overmind.

These feelings of urgency and loftiness are missing from humanity today. We are no longer inspired. We lack a goal and a direction. We lack the feeling of something greater, a sense that there is so much more to be done. Mankind is visionless. We have lost the spectacles through which to envision the divine. It is time to face up to our myopia and craft a new pair of glasses. For each man is ultimately responsible for the reality that he sees.

Recapitulation

PART ONE. We have come full circle. Starting with the void, the nothingness, man created gods and religions to fill the vacancy. The stopgap measure worked with mankind in its infancy, but as man matured, these "gods" (whether real or imaginary) simply stood in the way. They were no longer needed. Satan vs. God. Prometheus vs. Olympus. Faust vs. the whole universe. The illusions were destroyed leaving man in a vacuum. The existential abyss.

PART TWO. The existential rebels took over and held the fort, stood their ground against the meaninglessness, the hopelessness and absurdity. They partook heartily in the destruction of societal facades, annihilating all previous mores and values. But when it came time to create, the existentialists proved unworthy of the task. The most that can be said is that they knew how to sit and wait. Their intellectual, political, and social attempts at re-structuring were shoddy at best. For they lacked the energy and vitality to convert the rest of mankind.

PART THREE. The groundwork was laid for a renaissance of the human spirit. Human "culture" was fertile, ready to bear new fruit. The existential nihilism had swept away false idols, burning off the overgrowth, leaving the earth free and open to the light. What would germinate was anyone's guess. But it began to take the shape of the superhuman. Man's consciousness and culture evolved to the point of divinity. Man himself becoming what he had previously worshipped. Or as Kit Pedler says of Nikolai Tesla:

> In later life Tesla often said that he had no fear of death… he saw himself as a continuous and virtually immortal

creator of new aspects of nature.

Many writers have described him as a superman and in many ways the word is fitting, but not in a dominating or aggressive manner, but perhaps more in line with the much-maligned concepts of Nietzsche. A man who, by concentrated inquiry, continuous internal development and rejection of cultural values, is able to transcend his ordinary humanity and walk a little nearer to the gods.[198]

The circle is complete with man once again at the center of the universe. Man is in the void, but this time it is not external gods he will create, but rather gods within. Man will turn himself into a god, creating a reality that is voluntary and self-imposed. He need no longer look elsewhere for fulfillment, for the Metaphysical Rebellion has succeeded. Man has gained spiritual autonomy—from Childhood's End he is learning to become an adult.

The Gods are dethroned. But nihilism now threatens to undermine existence. Man thumbs his nose and stands defiantly against the universe. But it is easy to destroy, it is the natural order of entropy. The universe is running down of its own accord. What is difficult is to create. Rebelling for autonomy is only half the problem. Filling the void left by abdicating powers, rebuilding a new and better world is a task that requires Promethean strength and courage. Will we prove equal to the challenge?

---

198. Colin Wilson (editor), *Dark Dimensions* (New York: Everest House Publishers, 1977), p. 96.

"The Outer Limits"

"Only giants can save the world from complete relapse—and so we—we who care for civilization—have to become giants. We have to bind a harder, stronger civilization like steel about the world."[199]

The 1960's science-fiction series "The Outer Limits" had an episode entitled "The Sixth Finger" which dramatizes the Metaphysical Rebellion and shows a possible evolutionary course. The plot is briefly that of a scientist who develops a machine that speeds up evolution. A menial laborer is the first volunteer who undergoes the transformation. From dull-wittedness he learns quickly and becomes brilliant, surpassing the intellectual prowess of the original scientist. He becomes artistic and musical, composing and playing upon the piano, his performance enhanced by the growth of a more dexterous "sixth finger." He becomes the Nietzschean superman, as far above man as man is above the ape. But the inevitable happens. He begins to disdain these inferior creatures around him. They are ants and he is a giant, and nothing can stand in his way.

The evolution proceeds through a frightful phase. The "demigod" gains psychic powers over matter. With pure thought he can destroy whatever he pleases. Anyone or anything that annoys him must pay the consequences. The experiment is out-of-hand. The subject has run amok. The villagers amass to stop this maniac before he kills. In the emotionally-moving climax this evil genius goes beserk, is ready to kill, ready to crush the life out of one of the villagers who tried

---
199. H.G. Wells, *The Croquet Player* (New York: The Viking Press, 1937), p. 92.

to shoot him. But the look of disdainful malevolence in his eyes suddenly disappears. It is replaced by a look of gentleness and gradual enlightenment. He say afterwards of the incident:

> Then suddenly, it no longer mattered. I evolved beyond hatred or revenge, or even the desire for power. I could feel myself reaching that stage in the dim future of mankind when the mind will cast off the hamperings of the flesh and become all thought and no matter. A vortex of pure intelligence in space.... It is the goal of evolution. Man's final destiny is to become what he imagined in the beginning when he first learned the idea of the angels.[200]

A promising end. Or is it only the beginning? Science-fiction figures prominently in this last analysis because through it one can envision future development, one can imagine new worlds. The implications of the Metaphysical Rebellion can best be speculated about through fiction, imagination, fantasy and dreams. Perhaps one such "dream" will actually parallel reality, and therein lies the validity of the unreal.

All possibilities must be taken into account, especially those most distasteful. For it is often the most pessimistic that man is liable to forget. A contingency plan must be laid for even the worst case scenario such as the following metaphysical nightmare proposed by Mark Twain.

In his unfinished last novel, the bleakest most pessimistic of his tragedy-laden life, Twain has a *Mysterious Stranger* teach a young boy the ways of the world. The mysterious stranger is actually a young Satan (it is Mark Twain's *Faust*) and he fulfills every wish of his naive protégé. August learns about life, mankind, the universe, the spiritual realm. But in the end he learns far more than he could ever imagine. For in the terrifying conclusion August discovers what no man (or boy) should ever know.

> "It was a vision—it had no existence."
> I could hardly breathe for the great hope that was struggling in me—

---

200. "The Sixth Finger" episode from "The Outer Limits" science-fiction television series. Producer: Joseph Stefano. Director: James Goldstone. Screenplay: Ellis St. Joseph. 1963, Daystar-Villa Di Stefano-MGM Inc.

"A vision?—a vi—"

"Life itself is only a vision, a dream."

It was electrical. By God I had had that very thought a thousand time in my musings!

"*Nothing* exists; all is a dream. God—man— the world,— the sun, the moon, the wilderness of stars: a dream, all a dream, they have no existence. . . ."

"Strange! that you should not have suspected, years ago, centuries, ages, aeons ago! for you have existed, companionless, through all the eternities. Strange, indeed, that you should not have suspected that your universe and its contents were only dreams, visions, fictions! Strange, because they are so frankly and hysterically insane --like all dreams . . ."

"It is true, that which I have revealed to you: there is no God, no universe, no human race, no earthly life, no heaven, no hell. It is all a Dream, a grotesque and foolish dream. Nothing exists but You. And You are but a *Thought*—a vagrant Thought, a useless Thought, a homeless Thought, wandering forlorn among the empty eternities!"

He vanished, and left me appalled; for I knew, and realized, that all he had said was true.[201]

Twain's solipsistic universe may or may not parallel reality, but at the very least it exemplifies the feelings of those suffering from the existential void. When all values have been undermined nothing is real or of any importance. A bone-chilling emptiness pervades the metaphysical air. "What now? What next?" are questions that demand answers. Failure to solve these riddles will lead to decadence or insanity.

Imagination and creativity provide the only viable solution. Man into god, causa sui, the creator of his own soul. By becoming the "first cause" (if only in his own mind) man becomes responsible for his reality. For all values and purpose will then originate from within. It is the fantasy of childhood. We can "have our way." Whatever we desire becomes real for us. It is a godlike role that requires courage, fortitude, but most of all, self-discipline.

Man is at the threshold. Anything can happen and so man must be prepared. He must strengthen his will, firm up his resolve, develop

---

201. Twain, *The Mysterious Stranger, op. cit.*, pp. 404-405.

powers of awareness and creativity to withstand the encroaching void. Humanity is almost conscious, almost awakened from a slumber that has lasted an eternity. The first to emerge must be ready to fend for themselves. They must lay the cornerstone for their own solitary world. For only by being independent and indefatigable will their foundation be real. The English philosopher, Bertrand Russell, espouses these sentiments in his essay "A Free Man's Worship."

> . . . disdaining the coward terrors of the slave of Fate, to worship at the shrine that his own hands have built; undismayed by the empire of chance, to preserve a mind free from the wanton tyranny that rules his outward life; proudly defiant of the irresistible forces that tolerate, for a moment, his knowledge and his condemnation, to sustain alone, a weary but unyielding Atlas, the world that his own ideals have fashioned despite the trampling march of unconscious power.[202]

No matter what, man must never surrender. For the ideal man is a leader, not a sheep. The Metaphysical Rebellion has succeeded in securing man's soul. Will he give it back without a fight? Or will he stand firm and take charge? Regardless of the odds, the autonomous spirit of man stands fast, never gives an inch. The true rebel always wins, even if outwardly defeated, for internally his spirit remains unconquerable. From the first bite of the apple, man has been drawn ever onward and upward, his defiant soul prevailing, forever free and indomitable. Or as the English poet William Ernest Henley proclaims:

> It matters not how strait the gate,
>   How charged with punishments the scroll,
> I am the master of my fate:
> I am the captain of my soul.[203]

---

202. Russell, "A Free Man's Worship" from *The Basic Writings of Bertrand Russell*, *op. cit.*, p. 72.
203. William Ernest Henley, "Invictus" from *Poems* (London: MacMillan and Company, Ltd., 1926), p. 84.

"Jē´-s̈us answered them, Is it not written in your law, I said, Ye are gods"

St. John 10:34

Printed by Libri Plureos GmbH in Hamburg, Germany